INTENTIONAL TENSION

A LEVER OF VALUE CREATION AND GROWTH

BY ADAN K. POPE AND PETER J. BUONFIGLIO

INTENTIONAL TENSION
A Lever of Value Creation and Growth
By ADAN K. POPE and PETER J. BUONFIGLIO
1. BUS071000 2. BUS08500 3. BUS042000
ISBN: 979-8-9920788-0-0
EBOOK: 979-8-9920788-7-9

Cover design by JOSIE DIAZ-POPE
Cover image generated by Gemini, Google AI, 2024

Printed in the United States of America
Taraxa Labs LLC
www.taraxalabsllc.com
books@taraxalabsllc.com

Writing a book is a labor of love.
Even for the pages of non-fiction that follow.
Only with the love of their families and dear colleagues
can authors see their words come to life fully.

We were blessed with the precious time, skills, and
enthusiasm so graciously and selflessly bestowed on us by so
many wonderful people in our lives, including:

Debi Chernak, for her keen and conscientious wordsmithing.
Manuscripts don't become books without believers like Debi.

And our technology fellow transformation evangelists,
who shared their insights and experiences from the
trenches of M&A, including Beau Atwater, Andres
Siefken, Hongfei Ma, Ron Provenzano, Jag Siva, Mark
Mortensen, Farshid Mohammadi, and Smita Deshpande.

*I dedicate this book to my wife and partner in life,
Josie, who inspires me every day. There is literally
nothing she cannot do. Josie, you bring art, joy, color,
and love into my life, and I am forever grateful for you.*

—*Adan*

CONTENTS

Preface xi

Chapter 1: Tension Is a Feature, Not a Bug...............1

  Organizational Theory is a "Racket"............................ 4

    The Elusive Sweet Spot..5

    The Competition for Resources 6

  Breaking Points.. 10

    The Practice of Extreme Tension 11

    When a Team Is Pushed Too Far 13

    Desperation and Apathy...14

Chapter 2: Tension as a Driver for Sustained
Growth 17

  A Definition of Tension... 18

    Creation of Potential Energy 20

    Maximizing the Productive Use of Labor....................23

  The Entropy of Tension 24

    Sustainable Growth Enterprises 25

    Law of Big Numbers, Bigger Orgs................................26

    The Case of the One-Hit Wonder.................................29

  Intentional Growth 32

    The Law of Unintended Consequences 34

    Ignoring the Negative 35

    The Role of Principled Leadership................................36

Chapter 3: Tension Mapping 42

  Tuning the Racket 45

    Executing the Plan...49

    Know How Work Is Done...54

    Branded House vs. House of Brands 56

  Which Means That 59

    Operating in the Open...60

    Workshopping: A Discovery Process 66

    A Stepwise Approach 70

Chapter 4: Acquisitions—The Perfect Storm of
Tension..83
   Post-Merger Integration as a Tension Force Multiplier... 88
   Acquisition as a Stress Test of Tension Mapping............. 90
   Intentional Tension as a Driver of Value Preservation...102
   Managing Uncertainty 109
   Tune the Tensions, Don't Finesse Them........................ 114

Chapter 5: Principles of Intentional Tension 117
   Be a Weed.. 118
   Treat Culture as a Verb!.. 122
   Know How You Create Value 125
   Look in the Mirror.. 128
   Progress Over Perfection 130
   Transparency and Accountability...................................... 133

Chapter 6: Transforming Tensions 140
   The Q4 Blame Shuffle 144
   The Tension of Self... 147
   Quiet Quitting.. 148
   When Leaders Leave 150
   Amplify or Attenuate.. 151
   Digging Deep.. 154

Author Biographies 156

FIGURES

Figure 1. A System of Tensions 45

Figure 2. A Process View 47

Figure 3. Intersecting Tensions 50

Figure 4. Acquisition Antibodies 53

Figure 5. Branded House vs. House of Brands 56

Figure 6. Strategic Alignment 62

Figure 7. Changing Tensions Over Time 65

Figure 8. Order-to-Cash Symptoms 72

Figure 9. Order-to-Cash Functional Teams 73

Figure 10. Intraorganizational Tensions 74

Figure 11. Interorganizational Tensions 75

Figure 12. Tension Fact-Checking 76

Figure 13. Tension Sources & Root Causes 78

Figure 14. Intentional Tension Mapping: O2C Process 79

Figure 15. Order-to-Cash Current State 80

Figure 16. O2C Redesigned System Estate 81

Figure 17. SmallCo Professional Services & Single Product .. 92

Figure 18. Tension Stakeholders of SmallCo Multi-Product . 95

Figure 19. BigCo Organizational View 98

Figure 20. SmallCo as a Product Business Unit of BigCo 99

Figure 21. Pre-Integration Tension Planning 100

Figure 22. SmallCo Within BigCo Incubator 102

Figure 23. Intentional Tension Model 138

PREFACE

Tension has a negative connotation in the English language. In business, negative tensions can be observed in many ways, such as office politics, silent meetings, malicious compliance, and outright fear or anger. The intent of organizational design is the alignment of the company's resources and organizations to work efficiently toward the common objectives of the enterprise.

Interorganizational *tension*, while one of the most observable commercial forces that leaders must manage, in far too many cases, is the most troublesome to optimize. Why? Because tensions are often created by uncoordinated and contradictory, detached decisions—opportunistic acquisitions, insular sales compensation schemes, or subjective performance policies—that intersect with the most difficult thing to understand...human nature.

While competition between employees and departments or functions is natural, survival of the fittest inside an enterprise does not lead to desired outcomes. Trust is critical to forming healthy and beneficial relationships, both between individuals and across functional teams. But once trust is broken, it can rarely be repaired.

As the authors of the pivotal book on digital transformation, *Respect the Weeds: Digital Transformation Rooted in Principled Leadership, Vision, and Innovation* (ISBN: 978-1949642537), we bring our practical and implementable advice to the topic of interorganizational tension: what it is and what it is not; how to spot it in your organization; and how to apply grounded leadership principles to harness those forces for the good of the enterprise. Through a combination of innovative tools, use cases, and real-world experiences, we strive to provide you with an entirely new way to look at your business and how it truly functions. We will help you bridge the divide between intent and execution across high-performance teams without trying to boil a proverbial ocean of questionable business decisions or rewrite the human equation.

As with *Respect the Weeds*, this book is not intended to be a playbook or blueprint for universal application. We recognize that every organization presents leaders with a unique set of business objectives, competencies, structures, and cultures. We have structured this book to allow the reader the room to tap into their transformation challenges and professional experiences and arm themselves with the practical and transformative tools and methodologies provided. In Chapter 1, we set the stage by presenting an unconventional way to look at how organizations interact, digging beneath the lines and boxes of an org chart while challenging the reader to look at the true root causes and effects of tensions within and between organizations. Chapters 2 and 3 dive into the theory and impact of tension on an enterprise and its growth ambitions, as well as offer techniques to analyze and visualize said tensions. In Chapter 4, we examine the omnipresent scenario of acquisition as an extreme use of our approach. In the final chapters, we examine the implications for leadership and the considerations required to manage such fundamental change. Along the way, we will share some success stories and cautionary tales that we hope will provide the opportunity for reflection and inspiration.

1
TENSION IS A FEATURE, NOT A BUG

Organizational tension may be one of the most misunderstood management concepts. It is often seen as a bug in the system. Something unwanted that needs to be eliminated and the resulting wounds healed. But what about the organization with no or too little tension to speak of? Complacency. Lethargy. Failure to achieve goals and growth targets.

There are many books available today about relieving tension and getting everyone to play nice. This isn't that book. We see tension as a feature in the system that must be well understood, properly coded, tested, and maintained. Tensions that are intentional and productive can be a valuable feature of your business.

We have found that with the nature of human relationships, as in physics, there is just a "way things really work." That truth is revealed as you lead large teams across many companies and industries. Although the problem sets are different, the influence of ego and id and the need to manage the tensions of the business are very much the same.

So, what's different now? Why do we think this topic of organizational tension is important today and worthy of your attention? We believe that the days of "fast fail" have come and gone, and the speed of competition and erosion of barriers to entry have forever changed risk tolerances—in career risk as well as investment risk.

In addition, fast-moving markets and consumer demands are driving a growing preference for acquisition and consolidation over organic growth. That trend persists even in the face of failures to integrate businesses and achieve the expected synergies or returns on often sizable investments.

In such an environment where there is zero tolerance for failure, why do organizations continue to take the acquisition route instead of expanding with experienced and dedicated in-house resources? We contend that many organizations have not tuned their economic engines to deliver the competitive advantages and disruptive power necessary to support their growth theses. The potential is there, but the organizational tensions, hidden and obvious, constrain their ability to maximize the return on investments in innovation, infrastructure, people, and yes, acquisitions.

The organizational tensions, hidden and obvious, constrain the ability to maximize the return on investments in innovation, infrastructure, people, and yes, acquisitions.

The longer we lead and drive innovation and transformation for the companies we serve, the more we have come to realize that maximizing productivity and unity (cultural alignment) within an organization is really about managing the ebb and flow of tensions between people, teams, and entire organizations. After all, companies are, at their core, collections of people. As we all know, people have a myriad of personal and professional motivations. When aligned to a common cause or business, people naturally organize into structures and create cultures and practices aimed at social and commercial order. The collections take on names that we are all familiar with, such as sales, marketing, engineering, operations, and many others.

At the top of the structure sits the executive leadership team (ELT) and the Board of Directors (board), which sets the company's core values, mission, objectives, and, ultimately, targets. In a well-managed company, these top-level objectives are translated into a series of organizational objectives, and budgets and targets are established, all for the purpose of delivering the planned results. Great! This all makes sense, you may say. In order to accomplish anything of merit within the complex and ever-changing dynamics of a company, we need a plan and leadership to help us ensure alignment and execution and deal with the constant trade-offs.

The unwanted consequence of all this translation of company objectives to organizational roles, goals, budgets, and measures is competition and interorganizational tension! Of course, the business school literature tells us to "align the organization" based on a set of common missions, values, and incentives. In the academic sense, we completely agree. On the other hand, the real world of business is far more nuanced and complex. What if one organization may only achieve its objectives at the expense of another? Or the people within an organization see others as competition for resources or not doing their fair share of the work? Base-level motivations also come into play; for example, sometimes, people just don't get along and, as a result, start to question each other's motivations regardless of top-level alignment attempts.

In our experience, these and many more unproductive behaviors are the result of tensions between people and teams. Tensions are necessary and positive and, in fact, required to drive the work of a highly performing company. We need the sales team to constantly pull the customer view to the front. We need the engineering team to innovate but also challenge and vet the requirements and strategic fit of opportunities. If each function pulls on the others for the purpose of delivering shareholder value while minimizing wasted energy, then you likely have a highly performing company.

Unfortunately, this is rarely the case, in part because there is not a clearly defined methodology to do so. We aim to illuminate the sources of productive and non-productive tensions that exist within organizations and propose a system for not only becoming aware of them but, more importantly, aligning them to your business purpose and objectives.

ORGANIZATIONAL THEORY IS A "RACKET"

If you have ever held a tennis racket or attempted to play the game, or any racket sport for that matter, you will see that the strings are all under their own tension. The strings were all placed in the racket and stretched to a specific force (tension) by pulling one side and knotting it against a stationary point equal and opposite. This tension on a string may be considered to hold potential energy. The force excreted has created a stored energy that, when struck, will return force to the striking object. Repeat these strings left to right, and we have individual forces that have stored energy but neither contribute to one another nor amplify one another. This is akin to the departments within a company. These are the collections of people with their objectives, measures, and localized resource allocations.

Continuing the analogy, we now string our racket from top to bottom, being careful to weave these strings under and over the ones running left to right. These strings have their own tension, but they also now multiply and connect to the strings and potential energy of those just mentioned. We now have a tennis racket. The combined network of forces all act upon one another and have a combinatorial force matrix—meaning they pull on each other and the rim of the racket as well. (Picture the same for executive leadership, the common support functions within a company, and the like.)

Assume, for a bit, that this racket was strung by an expert who carefully planned the shape of the racket, the length of the strings, and their gauge (diameter), then carefully knotted each one while constantly measuring the overall multiplied force of the surface area of the racket. Strong but lightweight, well-balanced across the entire surface area, and easy to wield in the pursuit of playing tennis. It must feel great to have a racket like this! Regardless of the skill level of the player, this racket is a formidable tool in playing the game and maximizing the individual's odds of winning. The player is still the player with their skills and level of play, but this racket is a force-multiplying Excalibur, and when wielded by a champion—pure magic.

But what if an amateur built the racket with pieces of string, an old basketball hoop, and duct tape? That racket would not only be ugly and heavy but, frankly, embarrassing to play with. It would be more of a liability than an asset when facing any opponent.

For the sake of this analogy, let the opponent represent our competition. We came to play and win. We need a racket well suited for our purpose if we stand a chance of doing so. Before we consider the other many constraints, we will face in terms of our own skill level, the challenges of real daily business, and the fact that even though we may do everything right, entropy is real, and the universe (market) is a cruel and exacting place that cares little whether we win or lose, let alone survive and thrive. No, we will have to play the game and count on our trusty racket, a lot of instinct and skill, and a bit of luck.

The Elusive Sweet Spot

We won't go into the physics, although it is very tempting to do so, but suffice it to say that each racket has a "sweet spot" on its surface area. This is the spot where all the forces are perfectly balanced, and any object striking this spot will have the maximum energy returned against it from all the potential energy of our swing and string tensions. Unfortunately, the entire surface cannot practically be the best in all ways, so the goal of the professional stringer is to maximize the size and location of the sweet spot to give our champion the best chance to compete effectively and win each match.

So, too, are the dynamics of a company. Companies have strengths and weaknesses that accumulate over time and constantly evolve based on their employees, leaders, and even markets and competitors. It has never been our experience that a company is great at all things, and that is okay so long as the company knows and utilizes its strengths while diligently working to improve its weaknesses.

To maximize your company's strengths, you need to know what they are, and you also need to have a sober view of the more challenging areas of your business. In Chapter 3, on Tension Mapping[1], we will provide you with a framework for assessing and understanding the purpose of leadership's role in tuning the company tensions and processes for maximizing the sweet spot (competitive advantage) while identifying the sources of negative tension and releasing them to the extent possible.

To find the sweet spot in business, we must appreciate that while energy is neither created nor destroyed, it does come in many magnitudes and vectors comprised of direction and angle. Maybe you have a fantastic product you just released to the market, but the sales team is unconvinced of its competitive strength and value. They have a compensation plan that makes it clear they need to sell-sell-sell, but they can make their number on your more mature products with less effort, so that is where they continue to focus their time and energy. This is a very common example of opposing forces at play in product businesses. Each organizational unit has its objectives, and they look aligned, but there exist both positive and negative tensions that must be balanced to realize growth and market share year over year while still enabling the sales team to make their numbers and be paid for the performance they achieve.

The Competition for Resources

Imagine yourself in a conference room with all of your peers, debating and discussing the investments required to run and grow your business. The process is pretty simple and straightforward. Each leader or representative presents their strategic objectives, the expected benefits from them, and what their resource requirements

---

[1] Tension Mapping is a trademark of Taraxa Labs LLC. All rights reserved.

will be for the year. Assuming that the leadership team has established overall goals to frame the discussion, the task of each leader is to garner support for their projects and goals. Having participated in these meetings for many years now, we have recognized a pattern we affectionately call "Budget Bingo."

Leaders don't generally look for or even consider the needs of their peers and supporting functions. "That's on them" is the prevailing attitude. "If operations needs people, they will ask for them. As for my team, here is what I need." There is an obvious problem with this approach, namely, that great accomplishments are rarely achieved by any one person or team. In business, we truly need the entire company aligned and building goals and budgets and execution plans that cross functional boundaries.

As we articulated in *Respect the Weeds*, this requires a humble approach by a leadership team that has a shared understanding of what it really takes to succeed and run the business. If one team puts all its plans on the table and the other teams and leaders ignore the overall requirements for resources and coordination, expect a bumpy road full of all sorts of unexpected cost overruns and missed execution.

On the contrary, if the leaders agree on the objectives, choose a sponsor or owner, and then discuss and agree on what each team has to do not only to execute but execute well, noting what may go wrong and how they will address challenges, then experience shows that better and more predictable outcomes are far more likely.

The best leadership teams we have been a part of or witnessed possess tight relationships and mutual respect. In most cases, they act as both friends and peers. Who are you more likely to go out of your way to help: a friend with mutual goals and values or a manager you don't trust? It's fairly obvious, is it not? Of course, even friends have to hold one another to account at times. This is an intentional act of leadership to balance the tensions of the team. All members need to pull or exert force on each other in a manner that multiplies their collective energy to the greatest extent possible. In balancing one team, we may well balance large parts of the entire company. How do we do this? Well, it's hard! And we'll discuss this in detail in Chapter 6 on transforming tensions.

Big mistake: "It's just business"

When did we, as business leaders, decide that human relationships and emotions are not part of the business world in which we all live? Ask yourself: Do you know or trust anyone who appears to be completely emotionless in their business interactions, or, worse yet, is only negative and demanding? Not likely. People are people, and, as we've noted, businesses are collections of people. We all have emotionally good days and bad days. Pretending or attempting to remove our emotional side is a false narrative. If, instead, we aim to bring our full selves to the work we do, then we are, by definition, more authentic and intuitive as well as objective and deliberate.

We do need the hard skills, but we don't need to apply them as if they are the only truth. We cannot even begin to express the number of spreadsheets and fancy graphs presented every day in our lives, which are really just the overly simplified expression of a business. Hard numbers and financial reporting are useful when they are relevant and accurate. There is no question about this. At the same time, it's all too easy to confirm one's biases with select and static metrics and measurements.

Scorecards are an important representation of business performance but putting all sorts of other data into Excel for the purpose of making it look analytical has become a standard practice of management. A chart that shows employee satisfaction in a numeric format, without the expression or context of the company, is completely useless. Presenting a revenue-per-head calculation without taking the time to understand what work each team does, along with their processes and challenges, is also useless. How many bugs is a good number? The only answer here is: It depends on many factors, and understanding those underlying factors is just as important as the number itself.

Experience again shows us that by taking the time to truly understand the work of the people doing it, you cannot help but be more empathetic and, as a result (hopefully!), more human in your approach to leading teams.

Accountability is also key. But saying, "You own it. It's on you. Figure it out." should not be the first response when under extreme pressure. Accountability starts with clear objectives and roles and the acceptance and understanding of them. A leader may well have to resort to the above, but only in the event that after establishing clear responsibilities, the team doesn't embrace and own them. It's far more effective and, yes, more emotionally intelligent to discuss the needs of the organization, look for where best to place accountability, discuss it with the team leaders, and then ask those objectives owners to commit together with their peers. Once this step is completed, it will be clear to everyone who owns what, what success looks like, and, more importantly, what each leader must contribute.

Accountability in context

The concept of establishing "one throat to choke" should be banished to the scrap heap, along with the many other unacceptable business terms of the 1980s. Most of today's companies are technology companies in some way or another. Even if your company sells only commodities, they must be traded, and this trading is facilitated by technology. If your company produces and sells products, then certainly there is a lot of technology involved in making, delivering, and even charging for them. We still come across business leaders who hold the belief that technology is something "other" and may be reduced to simple metrics in spreadsheets—that they need not care about that and see it as just the sausage-making process. This is too narrow a view in practice. As such, today's well-organized company needs to be viewed as the tennis racket described earlier. Each organization has its role, and each leader their accountabilities within the context of the whole. The leader should not be looking for one throat to choke; rather, they should be looking for champions who can adjust and balance the organization to create even greater value. These champions must understand and appreciate both the numbers as well as the context within and work conducted by the overall business and its systems of tensions, rather than pulling just one string and waiting to see what happens.

BREAKING POINTS

It has long been said that people stay for the team but leave because of the failures of their leadership or, more colloquially, their boss. Let these be cautionary tales about the consequences of pushing an employee or team too far as you pursue the objective of tension management.

Clearly, there are times in business settings when we need to change quickly and adapt in response to a threat, or we need to really grind to get the work out. We all realize that just as there are seasons when we can go to conferences and take training, there are other times when we must just step up to the challenge and deliver, regardless of the obstacles or sacrifices.

As an individual contributor or senior leader, the choice to put in the extra effort can be very rewarding and lucrative, but as an organization enters this overdrive state, great care must be taken to balance the needs of the company against the needs of the people within it.

In technology companies, there are always times when great effort, risk, and innovation are required. Innovation is a challenging process at any time, let alone under the pressure of a project plan and customer go-live date. We have all been in those meetings when we realize that hard, unmovable commitments have been made. We then take on the task of creating a project plan on whiteboards and come to the realization that some extraordinary miracle of inspiration must occur that has never been done before that will enable the team to deliver. Often, this imperative results in leaders having to ask their teams to work extra hours and make all sorts of risk-laden and uncomfortable decisions, including prioritizing the needs of the company over those of themselves or their families. Incentives are important, as is the way we lead the team and the care we take to do so in a principled and fair manner.

The Practice of Extreme Tension

We once worked for a company that launched its products very much like the movie industry does. They would commit to a date and spend tremendous amounts of money to ramp up global marketing campaigns and advertisements, thereby necessitating that the engineering team pull out all the stops to deliver and hit the dates for the launch. Incentives were aligned, demand was being generated constantly, and as a result, the level of tension within the organization would likewise ramp to a more and more frenzied pace as each day passed.

These were the early days of the internet and consumer broadband being deployed throughout the United States. The team was formed and staffed after the market commitment date, and marketing campaigns were underway and tasked with tracking to a corresponding delivery date. The rationale was all about focus groups and the desire to hit the market with the hot title in time for the holiday season. The company was an arcade and console gaming company, and they had developed a creative studio and brand that was very much in demand. This was all well and good, but their reticence to take a product risk until they had confirmation that buyers would be intensely interested in the game led them to first sell a vision and then task a team to deliver it just in time.

As we hired engineers, we would also ensure they received certain supplies they would need to be able to deliver under the intense pressure that was coming. Those items included a sleeping cot, a mini fridge, a private office, and a bonus plan that would drive delivery.

The external marketing campaign was exciting to the outside world but filled all of us with an immense sense of dread as we absolutely knew we had to deliver against all the hype. And the hype kept coming.

As the leaders of this team, we created the plan, hired the team, and addressed each challenge as it arose... and there were indeed many challenges. Each day of work felt like a week. There was no time for meetings—just constant communications, living together fifteen hours each day, and a marching cadence toward our launch.

Every day started in much the same way, with a scrum meeting and a commitment from each team member about what would be delivered that day. The next morning, there were no excuses for non-delivery as everyone was counting on each other. If any commitment was missed, the entire team would suffer later hours, more risk, and the potential to make practically nothing for their time as the compensation was heavily weighted on final delivery and the initial success and reviews from key gamers.

To make matters worse, just as our team was committed and grinding it out, the same was true simultaneously for all the game title teams throughout the company. Contention for resources was severe, and leaders would poach employees from one another. You get the picture.

The stress of this company environment was so intense that it caused health problems for many of the employees. This was just part of the way the company operated. It intentionally created this environment and routinely increased the tension further through its statements and actions.

As our team had been tasked with bringing these games online at a time when dial-up networking was still normal, we faced a multitude of technical challenges and had to serve several game design teams concurrently, leading to pressure upon pressure.

The leaders of this team were constantly faced with burnout and exasperated employees threatening to quit. The reasons were all about the tension in the company, the external demand generation, and the internal competition for people and resources. Somehow, this all worked, though, as measured by market expectations and results. We delivered our network products, and the game teams we supported were all able to hit their market dates, too.

However, within weeks of market delivery, all but a few of the team resigned, the team leaders included. These departures represented a tremendous loss of experience in delivering a highly complex solution in record time. Herein lies the real cost of exerting such enormous and sustained pressure on teams and leaders. Loss of knowledge and experience causes inefficiency to creep into the organization as the same mistakes are experienced again and again. Furthermore, the risk of project non-delivery remains high, as the extreme focus and problem-solving required for success are drawn more from veteran staffers than from process documentation.

When a Team Is Pushed Too Far

Our best employees have options for where they work. In good markets and bad ones, top talent is in demand when it comes to technology companies. We may well see staff reductions and the ebb and flow of employment, but talent is the lifeblood of innovation and is usually in short supply. As we increase tension within an organization, it is imperative to be very aware of this fact and that our most talented employees often are our most principled ones.

This means that to lead great people, you need to be a principled leader and treat them with respect. While we profess the art of intentional tension management to drive the productive work of the enterprise, we are not advocating excessive pressure tactics but rather the most transparent and humble servant leadership possible. Taking the pressure tactic approach typically leads to a significant loss of employee goodwill, which, in extreme cases, leads to employees just leaving and taking their experience and talents to the market.

You will know when your best employees are all in. It is simple to see engagement and enthusiasm. When meetings become quiet, people become sullen, and challenging questions diminish, you have pushed the team or person too far. People are elastic, but there is always a breaking point, and once reached, it is very difficult to bring them back.

People without a clear view of their future may become miserable. This is just a fact in our experience. Our working lives are a significant part of our overall lives, and when they become untenable due to excessive stress and pressure, the impact is widespread and pervasive, affecting how we feel and go about our day. The best employees are the ones who care, and when the bond between the employee and the company is broken or frayed, the employee can become disconnected emotionally from the work. Staying emotionally invested while not feeling valued or in control is just too painful for people who care about what they do for a living. The result is usually withdrawal and resignation, a defense mechanism whereby the individual separates their caring and feelings from the work they do. This is clearly the opposite of what we strive for with intentional tension management.

Intentional tension management is about creating a positive flow of work and energy between people and organizations so they may do their best and most rewarding work in unison with the larger team and goals of the enterprise.

Desperation and Apathy

As the pressure ramps up and the culture buckles under the strain, a pattern, or cycle, becomes prevalent. This is the period between caring and not caring. We call this the "desperation apathy cycle." Teams experience a growing sense of desperation as they feel the pressure being exerted on them by leadership. The pressure builds, and for a while, the team works diligently to adapt to the new level of stress as they attempt to accommodate the new workload and reality. This can be seen very clearly in the example from the gaming company. There is a delivery date and an expectation of performance that just must be met. We don't get paid much unless both are highly successful, so the team accommodates the workload and adopts a practice of taking naps and eating meals at the office as they fight the good fight to deliver.

At some point, though, enough is enough, and the pressure builds to a point where a team or person simply cannot deliver. For example, let's say that the date for a project is shortened by a few months and no additional resource or requirement accommodations are negotiated with and accepted by the customer. At that point, project delivery comes down to simple physics and is subject to the immutable laws that govern the physical world. Unless there is a degree of slack built into the schedule, delivery on the target date simply cannot be accomplished. What happens then? The best people realize it and move to apathy. "Oh well, there is nothing we can do about it," becomes the talk of the team.

This is when a leader absolutely must lead. Leadership here comes in the form of recognizing that, at times, there are real limitations, and working harder will not always result in success. The leader must set realistic, *attainable* stretch targets and then live the schedule alongside the team. The leader must be honest with the customer as well and negotiate scopes and timelines the team can achieve. The leader also has to know when it is appropriate to (politely) say no.

Experience clearly shows that leaders absolutely must directly engage with and lead their team from within through a period like this. Holding status meetings will not cut it. If there is a design discussion at midnight, join it. If the team needs food, buy it. If you need to drive to a data center and help a technician rack a server, just go do it. No work is beneath any member of the team, including the leaders. Be an integral part of the team. If you have the ability to add resources, do so. If you have applicable skills to offer the team, bring them to bear in service to the work of the business. This is the only approach that has worked for us in times like these.

It is to be expected that teams will get over-committed at times. We should all endeavor to minimize these experiences for the teams we lead as the risks are often outside our control to manage, and certainty of outcome is not guaranteed. Perfection simply does not exist as it relates to innovation and the delivery of complex projects.

Tension is derived from many sources, internal and external, such as the need to innovate, aggressive growth targets, customer projecting their tensions, and even pandemics. In Chapter 6, we will address ways of optimizing those tensions. But first, we will need to dig deeper into the capacity of tensions, seen and unseen, to influence value creation and growth.

2

TENSION AS A DRIVER FOR SUSTAINED GROWTH

How are tensions created and destroyed? We view tensions as a form of energy, a power derived from the utilization of a resource that possesses the potential to create work. Energy is real and present in all aspects of the physical world and the relationships between people. Looking at energy through the lens of business, energy is created from the people and organizational dynamics that take place every day in all businesses.

If you accept this definition, then what are the sources of energy that drive people to do the work and apply themselves to the goals of the enterprise? We are all motivated by a unique mix of drivers, such as our individual goals, values, fears, and desires. The intentional actions, labors, creativity, and energy of people are the most potent driving forces a leader can enlist in the service of innovation and business growth. When human resources are aligned in a clear and organized manner with mutually beneficial incentives and objectives, their energy complements and multiplies, and the opportunity for true greatness is in the offing.

On the other hand, when people are misaligned, and their organizational objectives and incentives are misaligned, the result is typically chaos and wasted energy. Growing businesses that grow derive their power from the multiplying effect of their people. As a business grows, it is able to gain the resources it needs to fuel more and more growth. Eventually, though, inefficiency may develop due to organizational misalignment and lack of connection to corporate strategy, suboptimal incentives, and plain old politics, all of which waste time and energy. A vicious cycle sets in where the business demands more resources to grow, and inefficiencies grow in tandem.

Having worked for very small businesses, we have found that people are well-aligned based, in part, on the certainty of their shared fate. If we are a small team and we have each bet our houses and our children's college hopes on the business growing and creating value for our shares—*we are all closely aligned.*

As a business scales, more controls and governance are needed to keep objectives aligned as incentives begin to drift away from that shared fate and toward various business unit or functional goals.

A DEFINITION OF TENSION

Imagine, if you will, two people pulling on opposite ends of a rope in a classic game of tug-of-war. One party opposes the other, and the strongest or most clever and cunning pulls the other over the line and wins.

Extending this analogy to business, imagine a team of five people all pulling on five ropes against the force of five other people. Effectively, this is nothing more than five concurrent games of tug-of-war. Now imagine that we have two more teams playing tug-of-war, only this time, their ropes cross at 90 degrees to the five teams just described. As soon as the ropes intertwine, we have cross-rope tension. One party pulls, and an adjacent party feels the force as well as the party directly opposite.

Now, take this analogy and multiply it by a hundred. Imagine that all of the ropes cross in various ways at various angles and that those intersections change over time.

Given that we're speaking in terms of business, hopefully, the crossing points between our ropes are well organized, planned, and all directed toward providing productive work for our customers.

As we've described in our tennis analogy, force is not evenly distributed across the surface area of the racket head. Some areas exert greater force, while others exert less when in contact with the ball. The goal of the designer of the tennis racket is to maximize the potential return on energy across the largest portion of the racket head while keeping the entire system in balance and making it easy for a skilled player to use.

This is what we mean by **intentional tension** management within your business. The objective of the exercise is to do exactly as the designer of our tennis racket: to place the organizations (strings) within the construct of the corporation (the racket's outer loop) and cross them in a manner and pattern that maximizes the potential energy return for the overall enterprise while maintaining the ability for the athlete or leader to wield it in an agile and flexible manner.

Some tensions are, in fact, positive and produce a disproportionate return of energy. We want to encourage and maximize these tensions within the enterprise. These tensions create the work of the enterprise and multiply the effect of all the people within it to accomplish the corporation's goals. The best companies in the world find a way to leverage the productive energy of all their people and organizations in a unifying manner to deliver disproportionate growth against the markets within which they compete, while serving their customers and rewarding their shareholders.

The word tension, though, generally holds a negative connotation. We think of a tension headache. We think of people fighting for resources or personal gain. Negative tension within an enterprise or between people, we argue, is often an outcome of misaligned objectives, personal bias, arrogance, and the consequences of poor leadership.

Negative tensions will occur and are present within our tug-of-war and tennis racket analogies. These tensions must not be ignored but managed and minimized daily through establishing and exercising a cohesive and unified business plan, driven by leaders who exemplify a set of core principles, in the way they lead as they bring their most authentic and empathetic selves to the service of the company. Any plan is only as good as its implementation and measures of success. Implementing a plan is all about getting people and money moving in the right direction at the right time.

Organizational design and business workflow optimization go hand in hand with the concepts of intentional tension management presented here as they provide the tools with which the plan is executed daily.

Creation of Potential Energy

Energy is never really created or destroyed; it is only converted from one form to another.[2] As in physics, this is also true in business and the relationships between people. Think of it this way: Imagine that one organization creates a product. That product now exists but cannot be delivered because its billing and support are not ready and available. Billing is normally under the purview of the finance and commercial organization, while operations is responsible for the daily work and relationships with customers. This is an example of potential energy or stored value that, when released, should help grow the business. This is also an example of misalignment between organizations that, if not carefully managed, can affect company performance. You may be asking, how could it come to be that an organization creates an entire product and doesn't think about its delivery, operation, and monetization? The simple answer is that this occurs all the time due to the misalignment of teams and their respective incentives and priorities.

As we wrote about extensively in *Respect the Weeds*, it is absolutely critical that the company, its respective organizations, all the way down to the individual teams in those organizations who execute and do the work of the company, have a well-defined and coordinated plan. This is the simplest and most basic concept in all of

---

[2] According to the US National Aeronautics and Space Administration, the first law of thermodynamics defines the internal energy as equal to the difference of the heat transfer into a system and the work done by the system.

business management... and life, for that matter. Have a plan, make it real, and do it! Unfortunately, as an organization becomes more complex, people and their personal interests creep into the equation, and the need for a **unified and coordinated plan** becomes even more urgent but much harder to create, let alone execute.

From experience, we can tell you that it takes a daily act of courage and conviction to drive an entire company to accomplish a shared objective if the incentives of each organization are not completely aligned with a common strategic plan. Further, even if a plan does exist, it will only ever truly be executable if people are accountable for it.

We once worked for a company that was interested in product diversification. They were the undisputed leader in one very valuable niche category of technology—truly a story of solid technology leadership, focused investment, execution, and consistent growth. Having climbed this mountain, the leadership team was now challenged with an even greater challenge... to do it again.

Given that they dominated the market segment for which they were now well known, they turned their attention to the logical adjacencies to the value they brought to their customers. They looked for segments of their industry they could enter and still leverage all the strengths they had accumulated in sales, go-to-market, and operations. It was a logical progression of the company's strategy. Still, they realized they did not have technical leadership in the area they now wanted to grow and eventually lead. So, they bought a small but promising company in their target growth segment.

When one company buys another, there should always be a set of measurable objectives executives will be held accountable to as the justification for the transaction. In this case, all of these metrics were missed year over year for many years, as the new leadership team was not integrated or embraced by the acquirer; the displaced founder of the acquired company ended up leaving abruptly, causing all sorts of tension and unintended consequences in the remaining business.

People have choices, and highly motivated people typically are willing to make changes in their careers quickly if they don't see the opportunity for wealth accumulation and growth, as was the case with the acquired company in this story. The leaders were all told what the new strategy was by their new bosses, the tensions were allowed to build, and so much energy and value was lost within one year that you could not even recognize the acquired company any longer now that it was part of the larger organization. The vision was lost, and what remained was a collection of loosely affiliated, confused, and disenfranchised people ...and a lot of negative tension in both the acquirer and the acquired.

We were hired to re-establish a strategy and help inform a decision of whether to shut down and exit or double down and attempt to grow with a more aligned and thoughtful plan. Six months into the process, we had a decision in front of the board of directors: Our recommendation was to segment the companies into separate operating entities, augment the portfolio, and establish a plan for thoughtful growth. Although the plan was accepted, the company took another two years to execute it, and only then began to achieve its ambitions.

Why? The answers lay in this larger organization's incentives and those of its leaders. If the core business would invest one million dollars in their core products, leadership had high confidence in the expected returns and executives had a direct incentive to invest and gain the predictable yearly incremental EBITDA (a standard measure of profit) associated with this investment. On the other hand, the smaller portfolio had a much higher risk of return and higher growth potential but had not yet proven itself to deliver sustainable results.

As a result, core business leaders fought to invest in the core business, and we fought to invest in our growth business segment. Battles were waged constantly, with some won and many lost, so the growth business, predictably, did not grow at the expected rates. The organizational tension between these two product divisions was palpable and potentially destructive. The executives fought constantly, which created an organizational state of "us vs. them" and them being the "other," which consequently always resulted in poor performance.

So, what's the lesson here in this example? Climbing the mountain of success again is hard while you are on top. That's a lesson learned by many a leadership team. Beyond that, if a company embarks on a strategy to innovate and do something different, it is critical to align the incentives and organizations explicitly. Then, the productive energy or tensions pull on one another to achieve the company objectives rather than oppose one another and create unwanted heat and loss of potential.

Maximizing the Productive Use of Labor

The two companies in the above real-world story simply did not have the same objectives, customers, and, initially, at least, incentives. The acquired company had a way of creating product, marketing it, selling it, operating it, and ultimately producing value. So did the company making the acquisition. To make things even more difficult on the employee side, both companies had executives and leaders who, once the deal was done, were not clearly aligned or organized.

The acquired company produced its value and returns based on its people, plans, organizational structures, and tension maps (a concept that we will describe in detail in Chapter 3). When an acquirer decides to "align everyone to the central organizations," you can expect a loss of productivity as those central functions likely operate very differently and have very different constraints and capabilities. This led to a lot of wasted energy spent trying to figure out a new plan, operating structures, budgets, and accountabilities.

Instead, it would be much better and more productive to map the organizations and their tension relationships with those of the acquired company and link them to the corporate entity instead of replacing them! In both the short and long term, this strategy has proven to yield maximum productivity while minimizing damage to the acquired business and their financial results for which they were likely acquired. We will explore this concept in depth in Chapter 4.

THE ENTROPY OF TENSION

The only thing harder to do than to start and grow your business is to do so predictably year over year. Business growth is more like navigating a dingy in the Atlantic Ocean than it is keying in a simple hockey stick projection in a neatly formatted spreadsheet. When a team turns in a great year, the next breath from their investors will be, "How are you going to grow again and at a faster rate?" The more you grow, the more likely you will need to sustain more growth. And as you take on more expenses to fuel your growth, the need for money only increases. The balancing act of growing profitably is really the ultimate challenge and goal of the executive leaders of a business. Setbacks come, and costs must be adjusted; opportunities come, and they must be invested in. Rarely do you see companies that grow without expense and investment expansion tracking alongside.

We have undertaken this exploration of tensions, energy, and the flow of them to the productive work of a business because we fully recognize that flat performance is not good enough for most investors. Flat actually means *losing* value over time due to inflation, competition, and commoditization.

With a growth imperative set in motion, a company must establish a plan to accomplish it. In most cases, this plan will be a mix of organic growth of the existing business, internal investment in new offers, and inorganic options primarily from mergers and acquisitions, aka M&A. (We will take a deep dive into the tensions surrounding M&A in Chapter 4.)

Regardless of the mix of strategic options adopted to achieve year-over-year growth, one principle remains central: It is up to the people of the companies to achieve it. It takes all their vision, aspiration, and energy to accomplish this most challenging of tasks.

And this task becomes more challenging by the year as sustained growth is the goal, so it continues to increase year over year.

How does this happen? The answers lie in (1) the effective leadership of people and (2) a deep understanding of how efficiently the business moves from ideation to execution and monetization.

Sustainable Growth Enterprises (Hint: it's greater than single digits over time)

What does "good growth" look like? What number is the right number? The answer is that it depends on so many factors that it's impossible to quantify universally. The most important indicator of sustained growth is the fact that it has been sustained. To do this, one must keep the current base of the business from declining while adding new volume and lines of business to the mix without adding incommensurate leverage. To retain base-level performance on future operations in a time of high growth, leaders must pay even closer attention to their core teams and business operations.

How many times have you heard or even perhaps said of your core business that it's the "cash cow"?[3] Executing within the cash cow is not an easy or enjoyable experience. Cash cows are drained of their resources for the purpose of either profit-taking or investment elsewhere; or worse, they get slaughtered. This usually comes from systemic under-investment followed by an absolute shock that the business margins and market share begin to shrink year over year. How could we possibly expect anything else, given these constraints?

This said, it is inarguable that businesses and products have their life cycle, and, like all things, some must come to their natural end. The opportunity in managing your sustainable growth, though, is to not suffer declines in the core business (cash cows included) greater than the growth rate of the new additions to the portfolio of the business. To do this, a balance must be managed between the current core business and its future prospects.

---

[3] See www.bcg.com/about/overview/our-history/growth-share-matrix

That balance can be found through tension mapping, particularly when aligning people to strategy. The core business will need ongoing investment, to some degree, throughout its projected lifespan. The core business and the people operating within it must see an opportunity to continue to grow their own careers as the business evolves, and thus, the leadership team has a mandate to not only say that they "care about the people" but to actually do so by promoting leaders and bringing in new talent. This, too, is all about managing the rate of change to optimize the outcomes for all stakeholders.

Alternatively, bringing in an entirely new leadership team to run the acquired business signals that the future of the current team is not very bright. While keeping all the incumbents in place and not attracting new talent, the chances of failure are only multiplied, as new talent brings new energy and ideas and is a must-have component to growth. This all comes down, again, to effective leadership of people coupled with a clear and executable plan to achieve growth.[4]

Law of Big Numbers, Bigger Orgs

The law of large numbers in business refers to the challenge of maintaining growth rates as a company enters a period of ever-increasing scale of operations and financial performance expectations. According to *Investopedia*:

> As a company becomes bigger, it will experience difficulty maintaining percentage growth targets because the underlying dollars may become too large and unfeasible.[5]

---

[4] How do we grow organically and sustain that? That is the subject of our first book, *Respect the Weeds*, and is all about creating and rewarding a culture and process of informed innovation. Many of the concepts and learnings from digital transformation are related to driving growth and should be viewed as a north star for this discussion of tensions.

[5] "Law of Large Numbers: What It Is, How It's Used, Examples," *Investopedia*, September 23, 2022

We see a parallel here with respect to the size of investments required to operate a business that continually increases to a larger scale. Automation is, of course, always welcomed, but to date, wholesale systemic process automation remains elusive for most enterprises simply due to the age of existing technology in use, the degree of technology debt, and the lack of uniformity of business processes. Therefore, more scale means more people, and more people leads to more coordination, inefficiencies, and costs.

Inefficiency from lack of systems, processes, and coordination, though, is only one part of the problem with scaling. The people themselves and the tension they exert on one another, along with their objectives and personal motivations, as well as organizational boundaries, typically lead to massive inefficiency. Which only makes sense. So, have a plan, look at and align incentives within and across organizations, measure outcomes, and reward success. Above all, we must remain open-minded and flexible to adjust our plan as we learn more and overcome the expected unplanned challenges that always arise.

Let's assume, for the purpose of this discussion, that people actually do come to their jobs each day with their best intentions and aim to have a productive and meaningful day. In our experience, this is generally the case, and if not, it's an exception. So, if most of our teammates are coming to their jobs ready to contribute and make meaningful progress toward the objectives of the company, then why do we all experience so much conflict, delays, and burnout?

If we look at potential energy as the sum of the potential work of the enterprise and we look at tensions as resistance, then we may truly see the cost and waste associated with this problem. If it were easy to resolve, we surely would not have felt compelled to write this book. This is one of the central challenges of leadership and profitable growth.

So, what are the causes? If we can understand them, perhaps we can resolve them and realize the desired performance from all of our investments in people.

Even aligning two people with common interests and objectives is a daily exercise in ongoing communications and compromise. Aligning hundreds or thousands of people takes the same principles of leadership we wrote about in *Respect the Weeds*, and it takes an organizational model and plan to make it happen. Intention without process is just that in business: good intentions. We all have good intentions, but very few are ever really acted on.

If we seriously consider the implications of this "tensions" mental model, then every nonproductive tension that leaders and teams eliminate translates into an increase in the potential productivity of the business. This has genuinely been shown to be the case in our experience. As we have discussed previously, as businesses grow in scale, their demand for resources grows, and so does their inefficiency. We assert that the two rates need not be linear or track with one another. In other words, exceptional growth in business results while managing to add disproportionally less expense is possible. In fact, studies have shown that there is an optimal team size, and smaller is better in most cases. (Amazon is famous for promoting the concept of the *Two-Pizza Team*: "No team should be big enough that it would take more than two pizzas to feed them."[6])

Accomplishing such a feat is much simpler than cold fusion or time travel! What it takes comes from the following:

o   Practice principled leadership
o   Communicate, communicate, communicate
o   Automate the new (first)
o   Utilize effective organizational design
o   Employ effective interorganizational processes and metrics
o   Implement mutually beneficial incentives
o   Fiercely eliminate technology debt

These practices are all described in detail later in Chapter 5, but for now, rest easy that there is a tried-and-true approach to managing the challenges of scale and inefficiency. For now, let's look

---

[6] https://aws.amazon.com/executive-insights/content/amazon-two-pizza-team/

at some growth scenarios that set the stage for intentional tension design and the lack thereof.

The Case of the One-Hit Wonder

We once worked for a remarkable technology company that had grown rapidly and organically. The company was great at the one thing it did and the one type of product it sold. It was the quintessential one-hit wonder.

A dan joined the company to create a new, experimental product research group. The research would be focused on customer problems that were solvable and valuable to solve. These would be presented for the company to consider as it aimed to expand its portfolio and grow the business. The first part of the strategy was to create a professional services group to capture a larger share of customers' budgets while ensuring successful project delivery. The next part of the strategy was simply to create more things to sell and deliver.

The entire company was aware of the strategy and the creation of the research group. A team of experts was recruited, the process was established, and work began earnestly. Surprisingly to us, many within the company saw it as a threat and a source of tension. It was different. It was uncomfortable. The experts had all come from diverse backgrounds, and those working in the core company had all grown up together. The tension manifested in many subtle and some not-so-subtle ways. For example, to reduce the worries of disintermediation, a process was developed for the research group to create a detailed requirements document and high-level design that would be given to the development group to implement. But with time, lessons learned, and thoughtful iteration, the research team was empowered to develop data models and prototypes and sell to first-adopter customers. In the end, the research group experiment worked, and the company created half a dozen new products that ultimately created a unified multi-product portfolio.

The process was not perfect, but it worked. It worked because of the determination and commitment of a few of the founders and some good old hard work. If it were not for the aligning power of these individuals, this initiative would have failed at any number of points along the way. Founders have authority, and when used appropriately and at the right times, magic is in the making. Larger companies have leaders and organizational structures. They have authority. Yet a big difference exists between those structures and authority and the high-ground responsibility taken by a founder. We must lead even though we may not be a founder. Leaders who lead from principles and live them through their actions are proto-types for the cultural transformation of tension alignment and resultant growth.

In another example, we joined a company with a very proud heritage that had been systemically under-invested in for years. Each year, budgeting cycles had been the same for many in a row: cut more expenses to drive greater profits. Cutting expenses in a technology-driven company usually means cutting jobs and laying off people. This clearly had been the case in this company. The resultant impact on the remaining people led to the development of a *fear culture* in which management was seen as the enemy, and employees lived in "constant fear and skepticism toward leader-ship" in order to survive. Each round of cuts yielded less productivity, higher unwanted attrition, and even greater fear and skepticism within and between teams. Who could blame them? They were living a very real and painful employment experience. Why would anyone stay in an environment like this? Two reasons: a competing and more compelling fear of change for some and, for the vast majority, a commitment to the core business and its im-portant mission. It was work still worth doing even if the company's leadership had lost its way. Employees were deeply committed to and aligned with the organization's mission, and the remaining employees had become very tight, having lived through and survived all of this turmoil together. The team had become a type of family as well as a company.

When we joined this company, the most important skills we employed were to listen, learn, empathize, and get to know the people and the way things had been done and devolved over time. How can a leader have an opinion or form a plan to improve if they don't take the time to learn first? This also allowed the team to get to know us as well... to understand our principles and see us live them. It did not take long to realize that this team had simply been surviving in fear of leadership's constant pressure and intentional disregard of the challenges and consequences at hand.

So, what did we do? We formed the *team*. This step was all about establishing a leadership team from the various groups for which we were now accountable, as they previously had not been brought together under a clear and common structure. The next step was to create a point of view with the team about the priorities we would work toward. Then, we formulated a plan using the VSEM (Vision, Strategy, Execution, Metrics) model from Cisco. We put pen to paper collectively, taking into account our newly established roles and objectives. This was done in isolation from the larger corporation to start and, ultimately, in synchronization with it. Then we shared our organization, points of view on what we wanted to focus on, and why doing so would bring the business to the desired state of recovery, followed by growth, with the executive leadership team. Next, we shared it with the broader company.

Initially, we were met with nothing but resistance. We even changed the name of the organization, and for a while, people refused to use the new name. Over the next few months, through leading and living our new organization and plan, we started to deliver results. We gained a feeling of accomplishment from doing so and a renewed reputation for delivery. The broader company remained in a period of tremendous flux and challenge, but our corner was becoming tidy and focused on saying what we would do, doing it, and being able to prove it through our daily work.

The larger corporation groaned on and put constant challenges in front of us, but we had at least begun to clean up our own shop. When the challenge of cost-cutting directives came, we had a plan to compare to, and we could show the effect of such actions. When we needed more resources, we added them carefully or utilized staff augmentation partners, where practical, allowing us to create and maintain a new level of stability in our own workforce. This alone changed the underlying fear to an opportunity to grow, albeit with the reasonable and justified risks for any commercial venture.

Of course, as they say, the only constant is change: The corporation was then segmented, our organization was carved out, and new challenges were placed in front of our teams. The challenges required us to improve on and change the very structure and plans we had put in place ourselves. As expected, this time inside our team, tensions rose, conflicts arose, and we were faced once again with the challenge of leading. This was a constant work in progress, grounded in listening, mapping the tensions, and finding a productive way to get energy and work flowing again while minimizing the loss brought on by friction, ego, and the general reluctance of people to change.

We needed to scale more, find new ways to grow, and do this all very efficiently without funding from the larger corporation. There is no one recipe for this, but having a plan, communicating it, changing it, and living the leadership principles we espouse has never failed us to date.

INTENTIONAL GROWTH

Intentional growth comes first from intention. Not just setting goals and creating corporate mottos. It comes from really doing the work to think through what needs to be done, the value that must be created, how to organize to accomplish the growth, and, finally, how to do all of this as efficiently as possible. For some very select few innovators and entrepreneurs, the spark of growth sets fire and rages, bringing rapid opportunity and the creation of tremendous value. This is rare, though, and we are certain that for every one of these stories, there are innumerable others that fell flat or did not even see the light of day.

Intentional growth is about understanding or creating the opportunity to serve an unmet set of valuable needs and following through to the realization of solutions and value for customers who are so impressed that they are willing to pay for it.

Preparation is key. Having your company or team in good order is a must. If every team shares a common view of the objective for growth, has a clear view of what they are tasked to deliver and a thorough understanding of the tension maps within which they live and operate, that team has an intentional approach to serving its purpose toward the overall objective of growth.

If a team lacks any of these attributes, it is incumbent upon the team's leaders to get this situation resolved and in order. It is incumbent upon the executive team to establish the goals, allocate the resources, and empower each organization to continue to evolve an even more effective system of organizational structures and tensions that delivers the required work and velocity to grow.

This is really hard and almost impossible to do without a thorough understanding of how the collection of organizations **really gets work done**. What are the written processes, and what are the "real" ones? These are good questions to start with. So many times, it has been our experience that companies have gone through phases of growth, maturity, and retrenchment and have yet to modify their ways of working as they progress and evolve. What worked to start up a business will most definitely not work to grow and scale it. Should a business find itself in a period of retrenchment and cost cutting, the weaknesses in the organization only multiply as key people who hold critical knowledge and influence are no longer present and providing the value they previously contributed. This is when you really see the operational performance of a business. In a time of financial retraction, tensions rise dramatically because of fear of the unknown. At the same time, many operational norms become broken due to a loss of critical people who "filled in the blanks" in the business processes and tension maps of their organizations.

Organizations often struggle with clearly understanding the roles of the organizations, teams, and people, ensuring that all are consistent with the objectives of the business and clearly understood. If more than one organization owns a work function, then no one does. If a leader tasks two people or teams to get something done, confusion and delay often ensue. No one person may be able to accomplish a complex set of tasks, but an organization designed purposefully that is accountable for execution is the best practice.

If more than one organization owns a work function, then no one does.

The Law of Unintended Consequences

Turning up the tension on the racket strings to create energy and momentum for growth is not the same as creating menacing internal competition. Save the competitive spirit for your commercial adversaries. Organizations competing for scarce resources may be a way to let the cream rise to the top, but creating animosity in the name of resource allocation has proven to be neither productive nor sustainable.

One such cautionary tale surfaced a decade ago from a prominent consulting house in an attempt to help their clients who were struggling with transformation. They observed that enterprise transformation was hampered by the commitment of the majority of resources to existing products and services while new offers and models were in development. Their recommendation was to divide their engineering teams into two camps: a small, agile team would focus on innovation while the remainder of the team would stay responsible for regular upgrades and maintenance.

In theory (and in slick PowerPoints), this approach should have removed the barriers to progress by eliminating the propensity for business-as-usual servicing of existing customers. In practice, of course, it became a source of deep disgruntlement from the teams banished to maintenance mode. "What, am I not capable enough to work on cutting-edge research and development? Am I stuck working on testing and trouble tickets for as long as I stay in this organization?" The tensions were locked in place by these new fiefdoms.

The management teams who signed on to this approach most likely didn't see past the new org charts or the potential for unintended tensions they might create. They may have been trying to relieve tension between their strategy and lack of execution, but were they solving for a root cause of their growth problems with a reorganization? The approach may have made sense on paper from an efficiency standpoint but did not offer their employees' need for purpose, growth, and advancement.

Ignoring the Negative

The balance between our own fears and anxieties as people and leaders are in plain view of those whom we lead. Some leaders really don't want to hear hard truths as doing so often brings on even greater anxiety… or they simply expect their subordinates to "figure it out." We once worked for a leader who most certainly did not want to hear bad news. In fact, this has been the case more times than we would want to admit. As issues arose, we were left to resolve them as best as we could and only report back when they were completed. If a situation was out of our control, it did not matter: "Just get it done" was the mantra. If we could not do so, we were deemed a failure and likely to be yelled at, humiliated, and ultimately fired.

On one such occasion, we found ourselves at a monthly business review discussing the challenges of our technology modernization program. The leader blurted out in frustration, "Why do I need all of you with your fancy titles if all you're going to do is tell me things are bad?" To be clear, that question would be fair—if the responsible party has enough autonomy and authority to make the hard decisions about priorities and investments. But if not, then what is the point of having them, after all? When this was said, our reaction was simply, "Maybe you don't need good leaders if you cannot support them to lead."

Sharing brutal truths with leadership could also become a game of forcing the leader to make all the difficult decisions. This is commonplace and leads to suboptimal results unless the decision is of such consequence that it must be made at the top. Rather, when sharing brutal truths is accompanied by a recommendation or a plan to actually resolve it, the solution flows unimpeded unless the issue is too complex and requires a healthy debate about options and tradeoffs. Complaints and whining are not effective tools for building a solid, growth-minded team. They only create more tension that has no place to find relief. Sharing the hard parts, asking for advice, and taking ownership of a project or resolving a difficult issue: That is the model for successful peer leadership that should be encouraged.

We once had a leader with whom we could truly be open and honest. We could share the most difficult matters and push back if the tensions were rising. That leader had a tremendous skill: They listened, took in feedback, acted upon it, and was exactly the same person each and every day regardless of how hot things got. We truly admire this strength and aim to embody it ourselves as we lead in challenging times.

Leaders who can hear the hard stuff and remain true to themselves and consistent in their relationships with others are rare and, by far, more aware and prepared to take control when times merit doing so.

The Role of Principled Leadership

As you move into the next chapter, know that you are about to take your organization on a journey filled with self-reflection, empathy for others, collaboration, angst, openness, sacrifice, innovation, and, hopefully, meaningful and sustainable change. Willingly engaging your team and other teams in the organization in this endeavor will not happen unless they believe your initiative to come from a place of authenticity, purpose, and egalitarianism.

Tension management starts and ends with building *trust*. Without trust, there is no hope for change.

In *Respect the Weeds*, we tied success in digital transformation to a set of core leadership principles (see Chapter 3 on Principles for Transformative Leadership), including trust:

o   Authenticity and mission
o   Trust
o   Honesty
o   Consistency and positivity
o   Gratitude
o   Vision and purpose

Tension management will test all your leadership skills, ingenuity, and backbone—digging in deep, like a weed. In *Respect the Weeds*, we posit that people in any organization will follow those in whom they believe to be right and true and drag behind those they find inauthentic or not invested in their success. In our first book, we wrote of a leadership style that we coined as *The Undaunted Leader*. From *Respect the Weeds*, pages 36-40:

~~~~~~~~~~~~~~

The Undaunted Leader, able to persevere through the potential chaos and debilitation of digital transformation, would then embrace these key characteristics:

o   Bereft of ego and the need for accolades
o   Knows that the answers exist somewhere in the marketplace, in places that only a "weed" would find
o   Rests assured that the principles abided are more important than the destination

The Undaunted Leader knows the challenges will be large, knows resistance will be high, and is willing to do the work to form a point of view and to engage and develop their team. And they are not daunted by any and all of this because they know that by being undaunted, they will gain the support they need to achieve the results they will need to progress their digital transformation.

The Undaunted Leader knows the challenges will be large, knows resistance will be high, and is willing to do the work to form a point of view and to engage and develop their team. And they are not daunted by any and all of this because they know that by being undaunted, they will gain the support they need to achieve the results they will need to progress their digital transformation.

This is Not a Quest to Be Liked. Leaders are challenged every day to make hard choices, to take the hard road. To do what is right regardless of the decision's popularity. It is why they are respected and why they are often disliked. As a leader, which would you prefer if you could only choose one outcome: being liked and not making too many waves, getting along with your leadership peers and their organizations, but contributing incrementally and not fundamentally making a pivot for the business; OR, being as highly effective as you can be to steer your business to a future based on a breakthrough vision, driving the highest possible returns for yourself and your stakeholders?

I Know the Answers Exist. Undaunted leaders are visionary and inspirational—because they have to be. I am undaunted because I know that the answers I need exist within my reach. I may not know where exactly, but with thoughtfulness, research, engagement, and persistence… my team and I will find a way.

Fostering an Undaunted Team. Undaunted leaders will challenge themselves personally as well—to dig deep. At some point, you need to have the conviction to set and stick to your plan. We don't mean to doggedly execute a set plan in the face of changing new information—no, adjust your plan as you learn more. The goals are the goals. Those probably don't change as rapidly as the manner in which we proceed to attain them. The Undaunted Leader is confident in their ability to gain, assimilate, and utilize the bounty of information that exists around them and their teams. They lead from humility and a strong sense of purpose because, in doing so, they create the room for this information to fully come to light and be useful: to create a common understanding of the challenges and opportunities in the markets and customer segments they aim to address. Leading based on a principled approach further signals to the team that the leader is consistent, rational, open, and looking to lead within the team and not to simply drive them to some destination.

~~~~~~~~~~~~~~~

How would an Undaunted Leader approach tension management?

Adan was six months into his tenure as the CTO of a large private equity-backed company, where the stakes were never higher. His team had been systematically underinvested for years. Each prior year had been met with rounds of cost-cutting and increasing tension and pressure for growth. Improving the top line was not in the making, or at least not fast enough, so the company was in a perpetual reduction-in-force cycle. Adan was part of the turnaround and growth leadership team, where the mandate was to grow the business quickly but also profitably.

Adan had negotiated an approach with his corporate finance team that when his team needed more investment, they would do so based on new wins. He had also negotiated an agreement with their sales organization that he would help with growth by taking a more aggressive approach to product and technology risks. They would take on new work that took them out of our core product as long as they saw a real opportunity for sustainable revenue—if they could get investment support. It turned out that was a big *if*.

As he engaged with corporate finance, with sales by their side, with a contract in hand, they were told instead to find the investment within their existing budget. Growth expectations were already "built into" their annual plan. Mind you, the team had been cut year over year and growth had slowed in line.

Adan and his team were sent back to the drawing board. Needless to say, he objected to this new approach. They had a deal, they needed more investment, sales had come through, and they needed the technology team to step up. Adan's complaints were met with a challenge from the CEO, "I don't believe you need more people—you have a big budget, so come back to us with an accounting for what every engineer is doing in your team per product now and projected out for the next two quarters and keep it updated."

Adan's team swallowed hard. They examined every engineer's time and current commitments to customers and honestly evaluated whether they could stop any initiative or reassign work to the new project. They found about ten percent of the resources needed to service the contract. They had to create the most data-rich and substantial research-based analyses they could muster. With the presentation complete and the sales team on board, they were ready for the next round of meetings.

As Adan reviewed the work in the huddle before the meeting, his team was so stressed over the possibility that they would not get support regardless of what was presented. Failure would be devastating for them, sales, their hopes for growth, and potentially the success of their customers. After revisiting every number and chart, Adan and his team donned their proverbial armor for the budget battle.

The meeting started, and Adan absorbed the brunt of the skepticism and recriminations that started to flow. His team was texting him under the table about how he should be careful and not push too far. They had seen their leaders get fired for much less before and did not want this to happen to Adan now.

But Adan understood the sources of tension in the room. He understood the pressure that their company was under. It was not personal for any of them, as much as it felt personal. Leadership had just not seen evidence that this team could spend and grow. They saw the team as a cost more than an investment. Facts mattered. So did the math. Even with the endorsements from the sales team, and even corporate finance, to their credit, by carefully scrutinizing the analysis and throwing in their support, the game wasn't about plans or budgets—those were just numbers on a page. The game was about the trust that was needed to warrant precious resources. Tension resolved, it was time to get on with the work of building a solution for which the customer would gladly pay for many years to come.

So, if we see now that if organizational tensions are a fundamental feature of a business or agency, and constructively harnessing those tensions can be a driver of growth, how do we turn this intangible force into fuel for the economic engine of a business? How do we collect those forces, analyze them, optimize them, and operationalize them? In the following chapters, we move the discussion from the theory to the practical, with tools and techniques, use cases and case studies, leadership principles, and troubleshooting guides.

3

TENSION MAPPING

We have now established that organizational tensions can be both productive and destructive. Organizations may, therefore, plan for and harness their potential energy to create value for customers and shareholders, and organizations may suffer the loss of value from resistive or negative energies that impede their ability to innovate and achieve their strategic goals. How can you discern one from the other? How can you identify and describe these forces in a way that leadership can understand, coalesce around, and take action collectively?

We need a management tool. More specifically, a visualization tool. One that can capture the tensions at play, inside an organization and between organizations, so we can lay them on the table for all to see. We call this *Tension Mapping*. By mapping tensions, we can look for sources of value creation by reducing or removing impedances and identifying organizational disconnects where a lack of tension suspends progress.

Tension exists at the intersection of people, processes, and organizational objectives and incentives. Tension mapping will reveal opportunities for all of these as you explore how work really gets done within the organization at large. The act of intentionally examining and seeking to improve the workflow of the business likewise signals to teams that leadership is interested in and focused on continuous improvement and making their work lives better while simultaneously improving business performance.

In this chapter, we lay out a framework for tension mapping, starting with clear strategic (corporate) objectives, cascading organizational objectives and metrics, and how the divide-and-conquer operational approach leads to misalignment, friction, and a loss of productivity.

The framework presented here is designed to reveal three major insights, namely:

o   Retention
o   Attention
o   Intention

Retention. The goal and approach presented in this book are designed to preserve and amplify all of the existing and potential value and growth of an organization and drive the fulfillment of its vision. Every company is founded on an idea, innovation, or market need that, if well executed, has the opportunity to meet its strategic objectives and forecasted returns. Organizational tensions erode that potential, day by day and quarter by quarter. Likewise, a lack of sufficient tension in an organization impedes the economic engine designed to deliver shareholder value. Many legacy companies seek to replicate an entrepreneurial culture in order to reinvigorate their growth curves when, in fact, they should likely be trying to replicate the electrifying and galvanizing tensions of a startup that is scraping and fighting for survival and its next round of funding.

Replicating a culture is not an authentic approach to leadership. The culture of the enterprise is a unique and valuable asset that must come from the authentic leadership demonstrated by senior leaders of the team and be manifested in the engagement and buy-in of each team member. Cultural mandates and edicts may as well never be attempted. Dr. Peter Drucker, celebrated as "the man who invented management," is known for saying that "Culture eats strategy for breakfast." Drucker is talking about the real culture of the enterprise, not the inauthentic aspirational posters hanging on the walls.

Attention. It is imperative that we determine the root causes of detrimental tensions, not just the end-result symptoms or manifestations. Mapping—the act of visualization—places these tensions on the table for all to see and discuss. At the intersection between organizations, key questions must be addressed, including how each organization supports the company's strategic objectives, how they are measured and rewarded, and what they are being counted on to deliver to other teams to accomplish those overall objectives. Being intentional in having uncomfortable conversations is essential as it is the first step in formalizing what is working or acknowledging the need for improvement.

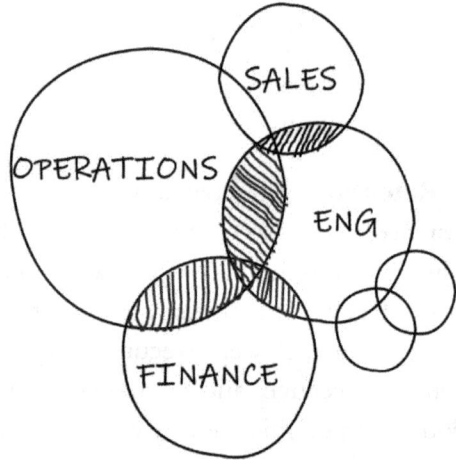

Intention. Adverse or insufficient tension issues can be resolved by effectively acknowledging the need for improvement and implementing changes to the systems of tension when they no longer serve the desired culture, innovation, and growth objectives of the company.

We will introduce in this chapter the Intentional Tension Model, which addresses the impacts on culture, incentives, policy, strategy, vision revision, and the like. This is the tuning of the proverbial racket, seeking value creation through the knowledge gained from the tension mapping, really knowing how the business works, and through enterprise transparency.

TUNING THE RACKET

Returning to our analogy from Chapter 1, the simplest way to visualize, or map, the tensions within an enterprise is to picture the various organizations within the enterprise as strings on a tennis racket. Interorganizational tensions are often at the root of productivity and suboptimization issues. As leaders, we control the types of management strings used and the tension we apply to each string.

Figure 1. A System of Tensions

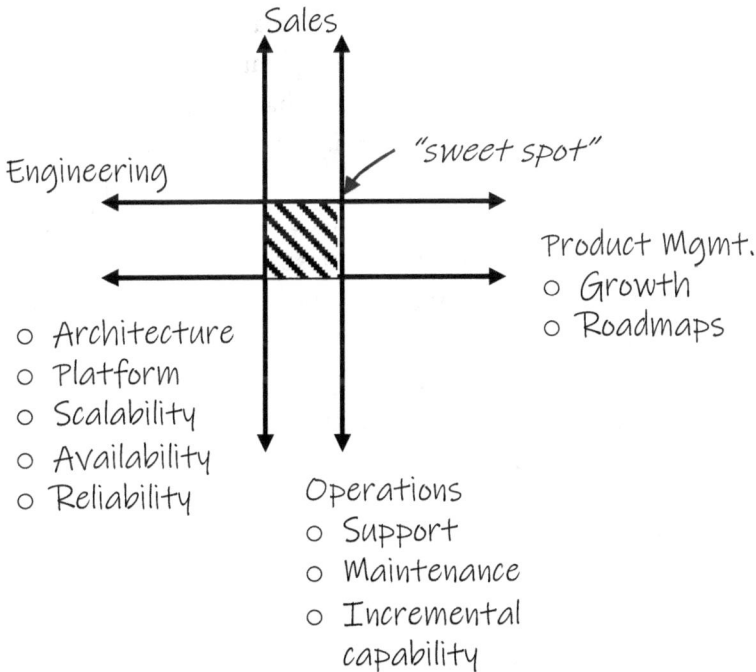

In Figure 1, the four corners of the inner intersections are the spots where the energy is stored and released. If you were to take a quarter and drop it on one of the strings, you would apply energy to that one string. But what is often overlooked is that the strings that intersect with that string will also take energy away from it through attenuation. In commercial enterprise, as in physics, that loss is often gradual and hard to observe.

It would be simple to say that we are looking for the "sweet spot" at the intersection of key organizations. Drop the quarter in the dead center of those four points, and you ensure a maximum return. But what is the maximum return in a business? Is it just the application of maximum force? Do professional tennis players want their rackets strung as tightly as possible? Not exactly. Most are looking for a balance between power and control. The tighter you string your racket, the more control; the looser the tension, the more power you will generate within the limits of string elasticity.

In our System of Tensions illustration above, we start to map organizational tension at a high level. In many, if not most, organizations, we know that Sales pulls on Operations, and Operations, in turn, pulls on Sales. We also know that Product Management pulls on Engineering and vice versa. Let's face it: Sales pulls on Product Management and Engineering, too, but for simplicity, we, for now, provided a simplified systems of tensions model. And, as we overlay the intersection between those two interactions, we also know that Sales will try to influence Operations and Product Management and Engineering. In many situations, such as a new product launch (a scenario we will discuss later), they will all exert tension on each other, whether directly or indirectly. The result is a mesh of people within the organizations, all pulling and pushing on one another directly and indirectly via their influence and organizational role.

Keep in mind that we're not trying to map every intersection between every organization all in one massive global atlas. The goal of mapping is optimization, not perfection. Further, we aim to keep the map simple enough to understand and act upon the insights learned. We aim to be intentional in how this system works not only today but how it could work in the future. If some organizations don't play a vital role in a new product launch, then they don't have to be included in the optimization analysis. If they're not connected, that may be okay. If there is no relationship be-tween engineering and shipping/receiving, for example, that's fine. There's no need to string the racket where it doesn't make sense. Isolation is a viable strategy.

To tune the racket, we need to know how work is done, what each organization is responsible for, and the capabilities and limi-tations of the organization; then, we create processes to optimize the flow of work. Tension mapping gives you a different way to look at the key business processes of an enterprise.

Figure 2. A Process View

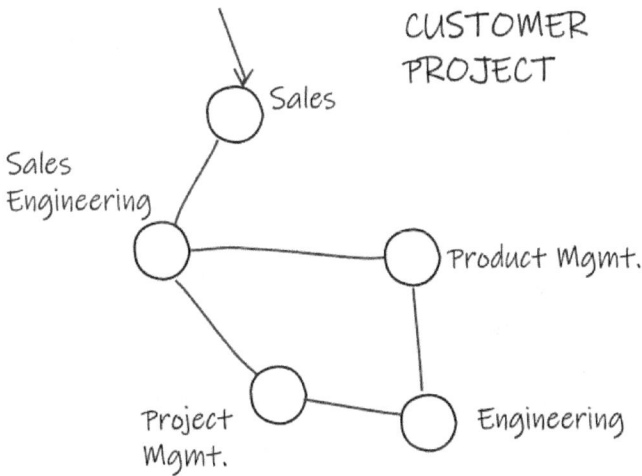

Typically, when we map processes, they appear to be linear. One organization hands off a step to another, and so on down the line. Such linear thinking often leads to reorganizations or reengineering exercises when a business fails to meet expectations. If an organi-zation's processes appear slow or inefficient, as compared to linear best practice benchmarks, leadership may look for cost-cutting op-portunities or steps to eliminate work within the organization. The results of such measures are often disappointing, with subsequent process studies pointing to newfound suboptimization.

Why might linear process mapping fall short time and again? Perhaps because it matters less what's going on in the circles and more about what's going on in the lines. Our tension model is designed to look at the systemic forces in play within and between organizations, providing leadership with the information they need to reimagine company structure, processes, and incentives, and ultimately deliver beneficial change.

It matters less what's going on in the circles and more about what's going on in the lines.

If you are someone who likes to employ next-level thinking, your tension model might start to look more like a molecular representation than a process map or Venn diagram.

A focus on interactions and enough depth to identify imbalance clearly and resolve it effectively—is all we're looking for in tension mapping. That's not to say we are trying to complicate things here. In fact, the goal is to be intentional in the analysis and design of the system of tensions within our business. Where parts of the organization don't intersect, leave them out.

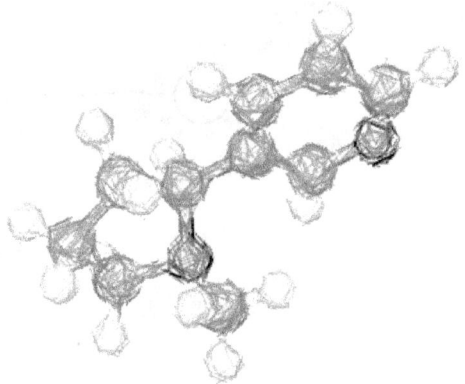

Visualize the company at the highest level and examine organizational intersections where they make sense. Look at the tensions that might actually improve the productivity and throughput of your team. These intersections of teams and the work demanded and provided are rich sources of value creation within the business. If there is no value in the separation of work, consolidate it. If there is value, optimize it for the function and for the overall system, which, as a result, will lead to optimal outcomes for the entire enterprise.

We have stated that the lines may be more important than the circles, which we believe to be true, but each circle (organization or function) must have purpose and value. Often, as businesses become more complex and encounter more complex challenges and needs, they add policies and procedures and processes to respond to the environment at the time. Over time, the environment changes, but the process changes never come, or they follow at a much slower pace. Being highly intentional about the way work is done and constantly striving for improvement is the only way to maintain the fitness of the business during times of change. And, let's face it, the only constant in business is change, so there are likely opportunities to reassess and refine processes and organizational functions now and continuously into the future.

Executing the Plan

In accordance with the concept of revenue retention, we know we must have a business plan, and we know when we either achieve or miss our targets. But is there a way tension mapping might help us determine, before the fiscal results are posted, whether the organization is primed to deliver (Figure 3)?

Are organizations that are supposed to be working toward a common objective holding fast in their fiefdoms and comfort zones? What are the *symptoms* of organizational or interorganizational tensions that are lurking around the corner or bubbling up from a misaligned set of goals?

Figure 3. Intersecting Tensions

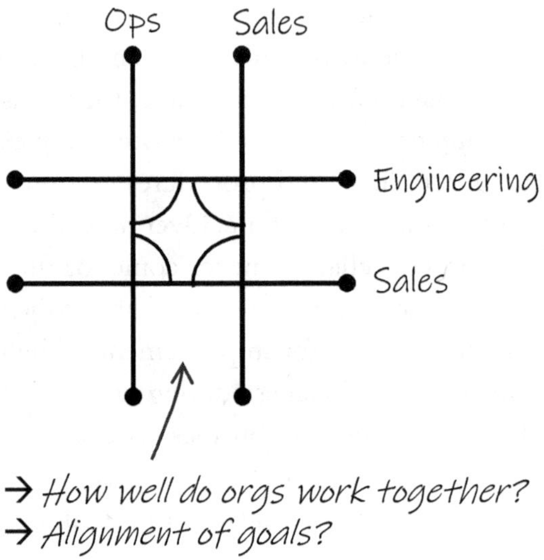
Ops
Sales
Engineering
Sales
→ How well do orgs work together?
→ Alignment of goals?

Symptom 1: Crosstalk

The company needs revenue. It must flawlessly execute to deliver on its full potential, driving the tensions between organizations to become palpable. So, what does the engineering manager say? "Give me the requirements, I'll specify a scope, I'll commit to a date, I'll tell you the price tag. Your customer will bear that price, or they won't; and if they do, I'll commit to a delivery date, and we'll deliver."

But if the requirements aren't solid—if they're not thoroughly or clearly defined; if they're not vetted with the customer; if they're not actionable—then all hell breaks loose, and we're in trouble. If the contracts were not written with enough constraints, that leaves us exposed to open-ended financial and delivery risk, and we'll be on the hook for an eternity of free deliverables fed to hungry and never satisfied beast of a customer.

And what are the sales managers worried about? "We booked the sale, so I need engineering to deliver, or we won't get the revenue recognition and compensation. Engineering doesn't believe in what we sold, so they don't want to commit to a delivery date. They underestimated the last custom project, so we either get hung up seeking leadership approval for overruns, or they try to eke out a product within the agreed-upon budget, and quality suffers. Either way, I lose all credibility with our customer."

All that mess gets thrown over the wall to the operations team. Engineering had to create a product so complex that it was beyond the ability of the operations teams to operate it properly. Engineering overran its budget, so they couldn't assign anyone to create the necessary documentation for the operations team to be trained effectively. Engineering complained that even if they did work overtime to write out the documentation, the sales team never allocated any funding in the contract for product training or technology transfer to the customer.

We're now beginning to string the racket, but not necessarily in a balanced and optimal manner. Sales to engineering, engineering to operations, operation to sales, up and down, left and right. This is how work gets done. How orders are turned into cash. How troubles are created and resolved. If organizations are talking past each other more than working through their needs and differences together, the economic engine of the business may not be firing on all cylinders.

Symptom 2: Microcultures

Some organizations we expect will have developed certain and specific ways of working. Sales will be aggressive and boisterous and lean into new opportunities. Engineering will act in a steady and conservative manner with perhaps the flair of an unappreciated artist. Operations folks cut to the chase and won't put up with nonsense. All are informed by their past experiences, good and bad. Many people hold on to and operate based on their negative experiences more than their positive ones. That reticence to think outside one's four walls can become so ingrained into an organization that it takes on a life of its own. The cultures within an organization, or *microcultures*, may supersede the ways of working that leadership is attempting to foster across the enterprise. People bring their biases to the table in subtle yet tension-generating ways.

We once confronted a product manager who submitted a budget that forecasted 2% growth. Two percent! How on earth could someone say with a straight face that they will work super hard for a year to grow their business by 2%? The corporate goal at the top of the strategic pyramid read G-R-O-W. They came to the meeting with all their charts prepared, investments and roadmaps, known risks, and mitigation plans.

And it wasn't just them; many of the product plans looked the same. Two percent, three percent. How did this team think the company was going to reach its 10% growth target if each of the product lines only grew by 2-3%? The product manager complained, "If I say I'm going to grow at 10%, leadership is going to hold me accountable for it. If they commit to 10% to the board and I miss my targets, they're going to fire half my team in a cost reduction exercise. So, I'm just going to commit to 2%."

Meanwhile, engineering has learned to present quality metrics that they know leadership won't understand fully. *Detect density per bug arrival rate over code coverage* or some such jargon. Is this a culture of deception or simply fear of tension and excessive accountability without control? "I know my quality is not up to par. I'm afraid to answer my phone when sales managers call with customer complaints. But the company has underinvested in our product for the last twenty years, and it's just easier to say we're focused on code quality than to ask for a doubling of our capital expenditure." Code quality might be a valid metric, but it is very difficult to translate into "Are our customers getting a good product?" The answer to that comes from so many things, including code quality, engagement service, contracting, and all that makes up a business relationship. Is quality getting better or worse? If it's worse, we take action, but if it's getting better and already pretty good, do we cut costs because our product is too good? Microcultures drive metric suboptimizations.

Symptom 3: Inorganic shoulder shrugging

Needless to say, many established businesses were formed out of years or decades of inorganic growth. We'll dive into the Mergers & Acquisition (M&A) tensions in depth in Chapter 4 but suffice it to say here that the challenges of post-merger integration are well documented. Like microcultures, your company is now a set of companies, each with its own processes and technology platforms, sales targets, and marketing messages (Figure 4).

Figure 4. Acquisition Antibodies

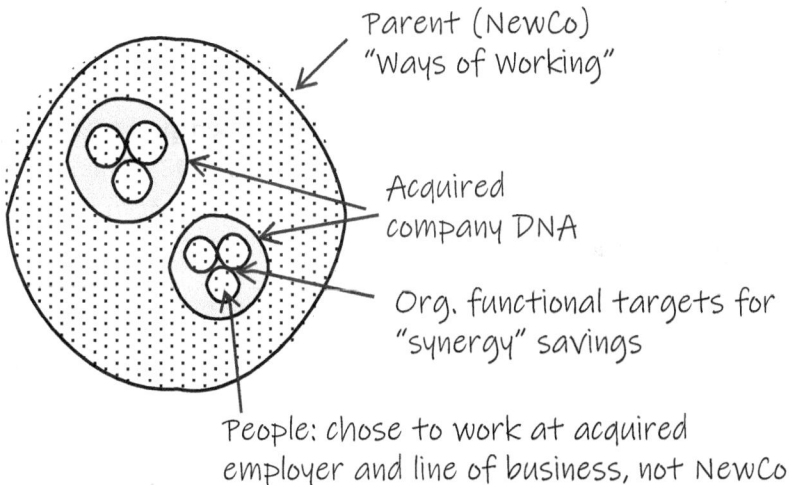

Parent (NewCo) "Ways of Working"

Acquired company DNA

Org. functional targets for "synergy" savings

People: chose to work at acquired employer and line of business, not NewCo

The tensions from inorganic growth often manifest themselves in the phrase, "I'm not sure." Can we build an end-to-end solution across our product lines? *I'm not sure.* What is the profitability of our inventory management offer? *I'm not sure.* What will the impact on the portfolio be if we change our primary raw material supplier? *I'm not sure.* "I'm not sure" sometimes comes not from a lack of wanting to know. The statement also comes from a lack of clarity within an organization, fear of stating something that later may be proven false, and/or the built-up tensions and inefficiency accumulated from poorly planned and executed acquisitions.

The list of tension symptoms is endless. The key to elevating and directing tensions is to be *looking and listening* for them. Sometimes they are obvious; sometimes they are not. Sometimes, they are in your face, but you don't want to recognize them. "That's just how things are" may become an unspoken agreement within or between teams. Or "A little competition between organizations will create energy and action." Or "It's time to reorganize the leadership team and get the blood flowing again." Executing on the plan requires more than just keeping watch on the numbers. If you get to "I'm not sure," then you're asking the wrong questions, and they are creating fear over progress. How about instead trying:

"We have an incentive program to operate as efficiently as possible relative to our cost of goods and suppliers. If we can maintain the same or higher quality and reduce the cost of goods sold, we all will benefit from increased profits and sharing mechanisms for employees. How can we eliminate waste and improve our costs of goods by looking at the objectives of each organization and the way they work and work together?"

Then, appoint a small team (no more than four members, based on our experience) to come to a recommendation that, if implemented, will improve the metric in question and drive improved employee compensation, and then celebrate the win-win for the company and the team.

Know How Work Is Done

Seeing the symptoms won't solve the problems unless the leaders and teams take intentional action to correct them. First, we have to find the source of those tensions. If we want a more long-lasting solution to stick, we especially need to find the *root causes* of the tensions observed. While no problem is binary, usually, it's either the wrong people in the wrong jobs or it's the right people set up to fail.

Tension mapping gives us the opportunity to step back and think about whether we have clearly organized our functional units, their roles, and their responsibilities. Have we aligned their organizational objectives to the company's strategic objectives? Are their metrics aligned? Does each organization embrace the objectives of their counterparts?

- o How are they measured?
- o How do they work together?
- o What are the assumptions?
- o What do they need from each other to be able to create the required outputs for the greater company?

As a leader, do you have a deep enough understanding of what goes on inside the engineering organization to appreciate why they get into endless conflicts with sales? Perhaps the teams *within* engineering aren't all on the same page when it comes to their financial objectives. Maybe engineering teams are still divided up by the different product lines that were acquired over the years, and they bring different points of view to the table when they engage with sales or operations.

In our view, being an expert in *the work* a team does is a must for the direct leader of that team. This knowledge, understanding, and expertise may be gained through ongoing and intentional engagement with your team. Believe us, they will appreciate you sitting in the review meeting and asking how things work. If you do not take this step in self-education, you have not earned the right to change what is being done and how it is taking place today. Ignorance and arrogance are two roots to, and causes of, business failure. We need to know—not think we know—how work is done within our teams.

Ignorance and arrogance are two roots to, and causes of, business failure. We need to know—not think we know—how work is done within our teams.

Branded House vs. House of Brands

To further our top-down view of tensions, let's back up and examine all the ways the company's business models are executed. For example, has a company that has grown inorganically adopted a branded-house approach or does it operate as a house of brands? Per Figure 5, a branded house integrates and incorporates its acquired companies into a single, consistent, and identifiable brand. A house of brands, in contrast, maintains a portfolio of brand images and independent messaging of each company post-acquisition.[7]

Figure 5. Branded House vs. House of Brands

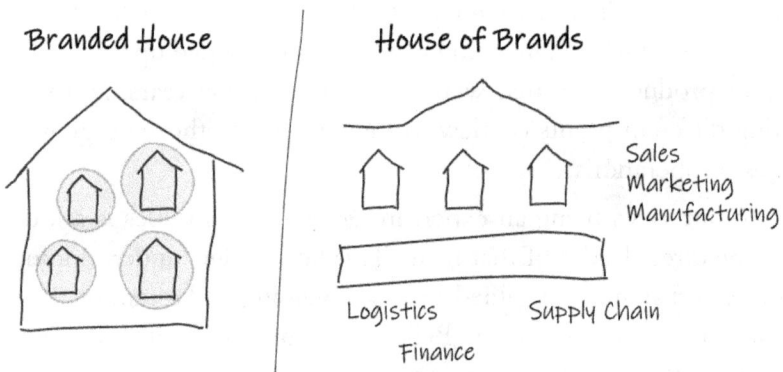

If you're operating a house of brands, the organizations within are treated as a consortium, thereby minimizing tensions between brands, albeit at the cost of a higher operating expense in maintaining redundant support functions. Their biggest IT worry, for example, might be to employ forwarding rules for corporate email addresses.

On the other hand, with a branded house, we're going to look at every organization and decide how to fit it within the enterprise.

---

[7] Our special thanks to Andres Siefken, preeminent brand transformation guru, for this model

That's going to exert so much tension on all players within the acquiring and acquired companies that we expect inefficiency and conflict if the integration is not deliberately and fairly mediated by leadership. A branded house approach effectively disconnects the strings of the acquired company's tennis racquet and attempts to connect them to the buyer directly without concern for the historic business practices or context of the acquired company. For example:

> We're going to take this string off and put on a new sales organization string, or worse yet, we're going to put the old sales organization inside of the new sales organization. We're going to give them common objectives to the incumbent sales leaders who may well take the following approach: "Hey, you bought a company, congratulations— you changed my quota, and you gave me zero additional resources. Now you've increased my OPEX by like 25 salespeople without the budget to support them. Well, no thank you—I am not going to work on this uncertain thing that I have no skill at whatsoever. I'm just going to watch it die."

While this scenario sounds like hyperbole, it is real, based on our direct experience.

How does an organization decide to be a branded house or a house of brands? Should they engage in a full integration of acquired companies or leave them as separate enterprises with separately managed teams? From a tension-generating perspective, neither is right or wrong. The best answer depends on how work gets done within both companies and that we implement the most appropriate approach that maximizes the value to both the acquired and acquiring companies.

If we choose to just leave it alone, we hope that we've aligned with the market dynamics. Consumers may leave the business if we change the branding, so we hope they'll be willing to accept a higher price point instead, as we won't have the cost savings ("synergies") to pay for the acquisition. We saved money with a full integration, but we have to hope that sales and marketing can mitigate the brand backlash. Further, it's critical that the employees in the acquired company see real benefits for themselves so that they can remain with their new employer.

Knowing how work really gets done will most certainly impact the outcome and success or failure of an acquisition. Mapping the tensions of a branded house strategy requires joint planning sessions with the pre-acquisition company to define roadmaps that are attractive to the markets to be served. During the due diligence of a target company, consider what the post-acquisition operating model will look like and walk away from the acquisition if the ways of working at the target company won't translate to a branded house model. The model you choose, or maybe the ability to change the acquiring company's current tension map, needs to be evaluated *prior* to launching the acquisition. Perhaps their corporate racket needs to be restrung to accommodate the addition of the acquired company to fit the desired cost and performance model.

Some companies we have studied have established a strategic function that ensures their tensions match their business model and go-to-market motions. Their sweet spot on the racket may not be directly in the center of their key organizations. Johnson & Johnson, a well-known and successful house of brands, appears to use their finance function as the glue that holds their brands together. J&J built its lifecycle portfolio (healthcare product lines covering everything from baby powder to knee replacement systems) through the strategic acquisition of leading brands in each product category. Their desire to maintain loyalty among these well-respected brands was supported by a rigorous shared services platform that offset much of the extra cost of organizationally independent operations. They tuned the racket toward finance, but not so much as to diminish the effectiveness of the numerous successful brand marketing and sales functions.

While Wall Street complained about their higher COGS (cost of goods sold) relative to their category peers, those same stock analysts couldn't complain about their earnings per share and sustainable growth.

WHICH MEANS THAT

Okay, so we've mapped out our organizations and identified the true sources of tension in the business. The tensions are clear and credible. We now need a way to begin the process of transformation and make changes that will drive growth and greater performance. What is the next step? Whiteboard the following three words: "which means that."[8] The benefit of tension mapping, of visualization, is that it allows us to *contemplate and ideate* a better future state of the business.

Here are some examples of *which means that* analysis:

o   Our sales teams are engaging product management excessively in every RFP, causing frustration and wasted resources, *which means that* either salespeople have become privileged in their jobs and don't believe they should do the work, or they don't have the knowledge to craft a proposal as is required for their position.

o   Sales is bypassing product management and going straight to engineering for product specifications for an RFP, *which means that* (1) product management doesn't have sufficient product knowledge to fulfill a straightforward request or (2) sales is selling custom work outside of the commercial-off-the-shelf strategy of the company.

o   Operations is passing every customer escalation to engineering without any site survey or real understanding of the issue at hand *which means that* engineering is constantly chasing phantom technical issues instead of improving quality and delivery on the expected roadmap of capabilities demanded by the market through sales.

---

[8] Credit to Smita Deshpande, Silicon Valley veteran and admired polymath, for this simple, yet profound approach.

By asking *which means that*, we're trying to quickly ascertain the root of a tension. We're not trying to boil the ocean or bring in a squad of consultants. We're whiteboarding. We're spit-balling. We're looking across our key processes, we're looking at the interactions between our organizations from an outside-in, customer point of view, and we're looking for the inefficiencies that are disrupting our ability to meet our strategic goals. We are working to optimize how work is getting done inside the functional organizations, the circles in the process, and what's happening along the lines that connect those organizations.

If we want to grow, we're going to have to assess, evaluate, and resolve some of the underlying issues of the business. Tension mapping is about resolving underlying issues of the business and driving growth by creating *intentional* tensions and doing away with ones that no longer serve the business. Asking "which means that" isn't a one-and-done step in the mapping process, as the answers to your query may not be straightforward. Different answers may lead to different potential outcomes and iterative thinking about the way you draw the organization and assign resources. It's like when your child is trying to understand how the world works, and they keep asking why-why-why endlessly. It can be a frustrating exchange after a while, but once the last *why* is exhausted, the child's query is satisfied, and your acumen on the topic has been thoroughly tested and validated. When mapping tensions, iterate, collaborate, and don't assign blame to the current circumstances. The goal is transparency and clarity.

Tension mapping is about resolving underlying issues of the business and driving growth by creating intentional tensions and doing away with ones that no longer serve the business.

Operating in the Open

Some companies operate sophisticated and sometimes brutal processes like soulless machines, while others operate like living, breathing organisms. Regardless of approach, all companies are made up of people with emotions, expectations, and ambitions. With that in mind, how do we tune an organizational "racket" comprised of people, infrastructure, and capital? In *Respect the Weeds*, we devoted a portion of the book to applying principled leadership and vision into organizational change (see Part III: Putting the Plan into Action). Transparency is fundamental to driving effective change. For intentional tension tuning, that openness should ensure (at least) that:

- Expectations are clear
- Needs are understood
- We eliminate the politics, organizational noise, and personal ambitions that are getting in the way of executing our business plan

Such transparency starts at the top with strategy and the recognition that strategy and its execution are at the head of the tension cascade. And, although we start at the top, we cannot just be top-down in our thinking and leadership. Meaning, that we set expectations at the top but engage the people who do the work on the art of the possible. You may be surprised how much better the outcomes become when you ask the right questions in a safe environment, where everyone knows there is a chance for them to profit from the company's success!

Aligning the sweet spot

That sweet spot on the racket may be as dynamic as the business itself. Over time, that sweet spot may move around a bit, such as during a post-merger integration or digital transformation. For example, the company may be very well-tuned financially but sorely lacking in IT and HR process excellence and tools. The key is to make that sweet spot *intentional*, where the tensions within are managed deliberately, starting with the strategy. We've all heard the phrase, "Not having a strategy *is* a strategy." It means you're doing stuff and hoping for a good outcome, unintentionally. And hope, as we know, is certainly not a strategy. We need a hopeful and positive mindset to accomplish anything great, but we likewise need a vision, strategy, goals, and an executable plan with metrics to achieve our hopes.

How might a company align its sweet spot on the tension racket to its strategy? Let's say we have a strategy to increase market share for our top three products by 15%. That's probably going to impact sales, operations, engineering, and marketing. It's going to put tension on all four of those organizations to deliver (Figure 6).

Figure 6. Strategic Alignment

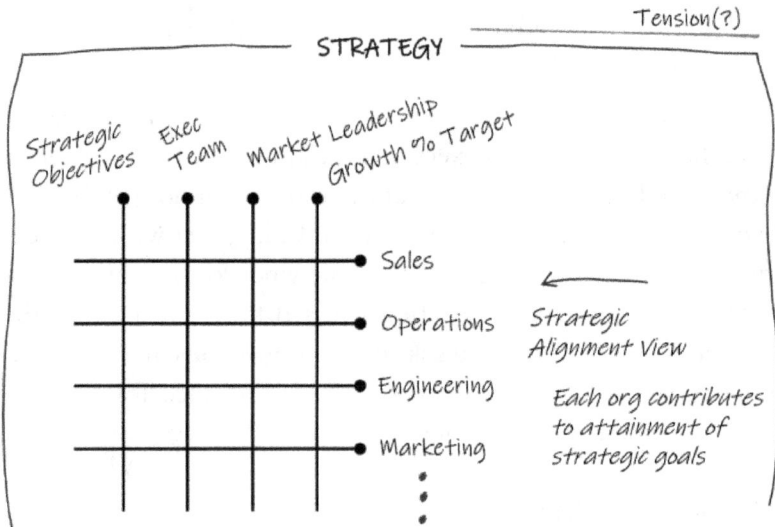

Likewise, if we have a strategy to consolidate many vendors to achieve economies of scale, it's probably going to impact finance and engineering. If we have a strategy to outsource operations to lower cost, it's going to impact operations and also possibly sales. And, if we have a market leadership strategy, it's going to be all about sales and marketing as the company asserts its position in the market.

Start by knowing the cultures of each of these organizations and the tensions they will bring to the table—*all of the tensions* they will bring to the table. Where should we place the sweet spot, intentionally, for each of these strategies? Do we try to change the microcultures with each new strategic intent, or do we tune the racket to balance the enterprise response to meet our objectives? Are we forever managing the ingrained experiences and reticence toward change, or can we set up the company to be successful no matter how grand our strategic intent may be?

Organizational discipline

Leaders often complain that their teams aren't disciplined enough. The word *lassitude* (lack of motivation, weariness) sits on the whiteboard parking lot at every meeting with HR leadership. What were the choices? "You either train them, or you fire them." You train them, they accept the training, or you decide that they can't do it, and you fire them.

Which means that—our organizational discipline issue might come from a lack of understanding of the tensions within the organization, organizational learning, and process improvement. That's it. That's all you have, really. Transparency. Either your teams know what they are accountable for, they know what the inputs and the outputs are, they know how others depend upon them, or they don't.

In order to tune an organization, we need to establish clear norms and working processes to make working together as efficient and actionable as possible, given the constraints we have. Tuning the racket is knowing how the work is done, knowing what each organization is responsible for, knowing the capacities and limitations of the organizations, and creating processes to optimize the flow of work.

How might we apply this to the interorganizational tension symptoms we discussed earlier? How do we resolve the dysfunction between sales and product management and all the scar tissue that's built up over the years from a lack of transparency or accountability? Product management claims they don't have enough training time to support the sales teams effectively. Well, that's no excuse! Let's hash it out and create a new product introduction process. We'll then take our action items and post them outside the conference room doors. Now we have accountability, right?

Your sales engineers are accountable within the scope of these products to specify and respond to RFPs, work with customers, and do whatever else is necessary for us to win business. If it's outside of that scope, let's set up a new Architecture Council to manage scope creep and out-of-cycle feature change.

How does something like an architecture council address or mitigate tensions? As leaders, we're creating a common set of standards and processes within an organization and an environment where decisions are uniformly applied across any fiefdoms within a team or silos between teams. We may also be building better mousetraps so that we have a way for people to say they disagree with a new standard, process, or solutions architecture, etc. If they disagree, great! Challenging norms is a cultural attribute of continual improvement and learning. The aim should be to act toward one another in an egalitarian manner, debate the idea, and make the best decision based on the best information we have from the team. That alone will move the culture in a positive and productivity-boosting manner. If a team member has a better and substantiated idea that will make something better, we will take it, implement it, and iterate toward a better future.

Beyond that rigor, an architecture council exerts tension across the entire organization in a constructive manner. The objective is to create more unified and better outcomes for our employees, our business, and our customers. We want cohesion across technologies and offerings because, in the end, our customers don't care whatsoever if what they are buying is a bundle of acquired products from a house of brands or not. They just want a valuable, secure, and reliable offer at a price that fits the market.

Managing the ebb and flow of tensions

The balance of organizational forces and tension may change over time, even within the course of a project or program. A new product introduction is a great example of how transparency between organizations translates into a clear understanding of where the racket may be intentionally tuned over time (Figure 7).

Figure 7. Changing Tensions Over Time

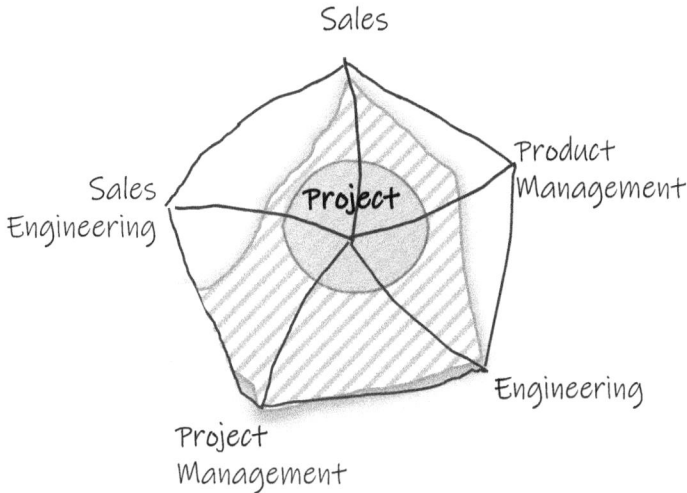

If we look at a tension map as an area diagram—we know, bear with us—we might start to visualize the ebb and flow of organizational authority and expectations over the course of a product launch. Instead of the organizations pulling against each other equally at the center of the project, each understands that contributions will vary as the project progresses. Sales may have a tangential role at the beginning of gathering market intelligence for product management and engineering. As the launch progresses, their role grows until the point that they dominate the project, and the other organizations become more aligned to the workflow motions of the sales team.

If every organization believes they are the center of attention throughout the project, then we have a problem. Likewise, if one organization is exerting *all* the pressure on all the organizations, we also probably have a problem (which means that), as the creators of valuable work product and the receivers of it are not measured on the delivery of it, or they are not measured in a unified way (e.g., expressed in increased business performance). If the engineering team controls a new product introduction from ideation to customer installation, the offering likely will not meet the full needs of the customer. We need the energy and direction from product marketing, customer service, and sales to ensure success.

If every organization believes they are the center of attention throughout the project, then we have a problem.

Workshopping: A Discovery Process

Tension mapping is meant to be a process of discovery that yields real improvements in the organization and operation of a business. It is different than basic process mapping in that it is intended to capture the organizational roles and responsibilities as well as the workflow and tensions between the related organizations of a business. Once this process is conducted, it is further intended to be used as an educational tool and an active operational model for leaders who cross organizational and process boundaries to engage in continuous learning and improvement.

As a leader, the outcome of tension mapping provides a powerful tool that is intended to enable the active management of tension to create growth, balanced with a positive and creative work culture where the individual, as well as the organization, are well served over the long term.

Consider the simple model below as a blueprint for conducting tension mapping. Change what you feel is appropriate for your environment. That said, our experience has proven that this model is highly effective as a starting point to understand and begin to become intentional about the tensions in the companies to which we have applied it.

- o Objective: We seek to create an understanding of what each team does and how they interact with one another to provide value to the overall business for the purpose of maximizing productive work while eliminating unnecessary tension and waste.
- o Method: We address this objective by developing a visual diagram (tension map) that represents the structure and relationships of teams of people organized to accomplish work within an organizational unit. The unit may be the entire company, a department, a team, or a task-level function.

Workshop structure

Tension mapping is intended to be performed in a facilitated pair of workshops. It is critically important that the two workshops be separated, as experience has shown that attempting to do everything in one session tends to yield more chaos than active listening and understanding. Change is difficult; therefore, we propose separating the current state discussion from the future state discussion to give participants the opportunity to truly understand the way things are in a neutral setting without blame and politics entering into the process.

- ◊ Phase 1: *The Way Things Are Session*. This session focuses on cataloging the current state and producing a true representation of the business as it is intended to and actually operates between organizations.

- ◊ Phase 2: *Tension Balancing Session*. This session focuses on eliminating waste, unnecessary loops, steps, and unproductive tensions.

Mapping symbols:

A: Open circle: Represents a team of people performing defined work.

B: Solid arc: Represents an intentional connection between teams of people. The key word here is intentional.

C: Dashed arc: Represents a de facto or "the way things really work" connection between teams of people.

D: Arrows: Arrows are placed on the Arcs to represent the direction of workflow between teams. These directions may be to, from, or bidirectional.

E: Document: Represents a work item produced in the execution of a business process that moves between work groups.

F: Plus sign (+) within a circle: Represents the beginning of a process.

G: Negative sign (-) within a circle: Represents the end of a process.

Rules of Engagement:
1) Secure senior leadership buy-in prior to conducting this work (imperative)
2) Display mutual respect and active listening at all times
3) No politics, blame, guilt, or defensiveness
4) Pose objective, open-ended questions only (no leading questions)
5) Place items that come up but fall outside the scope of the session in the parking lot and resolve them separately

Participants:
1) Sponsor: senior leader (or a delegate depending on the scope of the exercise) who is accountable for the business processes within the scope and has the authority to implement recommendations
2) Team leaders accountable for the organizations in scope

3) Key team members who do the work and can speak to the intended and actual processes of each team

4) Facilitator: a neutral person who conducts the tension mapping meetings and ensures that politics and defensiveness are avoided

Session 1: The Way Things Are

1) Senior leader sponsor establishes the scope of the tension map based on criticality and makes clear that the goal in this phase of the process is *simply to understand*. There is no analysis or judgment in this phase.

2) Senior leader sponsor identifies representatives of the designated teams who can speak to the manner in which they work and how their team relates to the overall business.

3) Facilitator reviews the rules of engagement and the symbols.

4) Define the desired objective outcomes from optimization of the tension map being developed.

5) Each team shares amongst themselves and writes down what they are accountable for.

6) Facilitator draws each organization on the board, noting inputs and outputs of what they produce (does not connect the organizations until all circles are drawn and defined).

    a. Asks "Who requests and who receives?" for each input or output workflow.

    b. Using this information, draws solid and dashed arcs illustrating the connections between each of the organizations.

This will take time. Be patient and be open to the known and unknown problems. As concerns come up, note them but do not resolve them.

7) Facilitator documents everything and schedules Tension Balancing session in a timely manner.

Session 2: Tension Balancing

1) Meeting includes the same participants as Session 1.

2) Facilitator opens the meeting with the "Way Thing Are" map by reviewing the connections one at a time, focusing on the movement of documents and loops, and asking

open-ended questions including: "Is this how we want the organization to work?" "Who owns the ultimate outcome of the process?" "What happens when?" And "How might we...?"

3) Suggested approach: Facilitator separates participants into pairs of teams, each of which is tasked with considering all of the input from the sessions and proposing how to balance the tensions in a manner that will yield better outcomes. Facilitator then brings the teams together to share and discuss their recommendations.

4) Iterate, experiment, balance, and empower the teams to shape the future of work within and between their teams!

5) As with all experiments, state the thesis of the intended experiment and measure the results to ensure the objectives were achieved. (For example, introducing an AI chatbot to the core product will increase customer interaction by 10%.)

A Stepwise Approach

In our experience, visualization is the very best way to identify, analyze, and communicate what you believe with others. Our work and analyses need to be detectable, observable, and articulable. So far in this chapter, we have presented a stepwise framework to visualize your organizations, the tensions within and between, and take proactive steps to work towards better outcomes.

The tension mapping framework lends itself to a more easily managed, stepwise approach:

o Clearly define your organizational (functional) units.
o Articulate clear strategic objectives, aligned with senior leadership.
o Develop clear organizational objectives that align with the company's strategic plan or objectives.
o Document transparent operational metrics and processes within each organization.
o Specify the optimal intersections between organizations ("We expect that...").

- o Evaluate the resulting tensions, including:
  - Can each organization support the strategic objective without creating undue tensions?
  - Can each organization clearly articulate and embrace the objectives of their intersecting organizations?
  - How are we measuring productive and unproductive tension?

Let's walk through a simple example. Say an organization is struggling with its order-to-cash process (which includes order management, fulfillment, invoicing, payment, etc.). The CFO has noticed cash flow issues that seem to relate to billing inaccuracies and slow payments. When the issue is raised at a finance managers' meeting, all hell breaks loose. "Cash flow is the end result of about two dozen short-sighted initiatives from our *Get SaaSy* mandate from your last leadership retreat, where we're supposed to be taking crypto for payments as a marketing ploy, and our new product line is now targeted at a higher-credit-risk clientele; meanwhile half of our SKUs on that line are out of stock and the other half aren't selling yet.

After some investigation with the rest of the leadership team, the CFO calls for a workshop with key team leaders within finance, customer care, IT, and operations. Following a discussion of desired outcomes and the rules of engagement, the workshop group begins to map out the way things are, starting with an understanding of the process… just to make sure everyone is on the same page (Figure 8). Before one marker was even picked up, the workshop group agreed that they were not searching for "technology panaceas" out of this exercise. That approach had been tried—and failed—many times before.

Figure 8. Order-to-Cash Symptoms

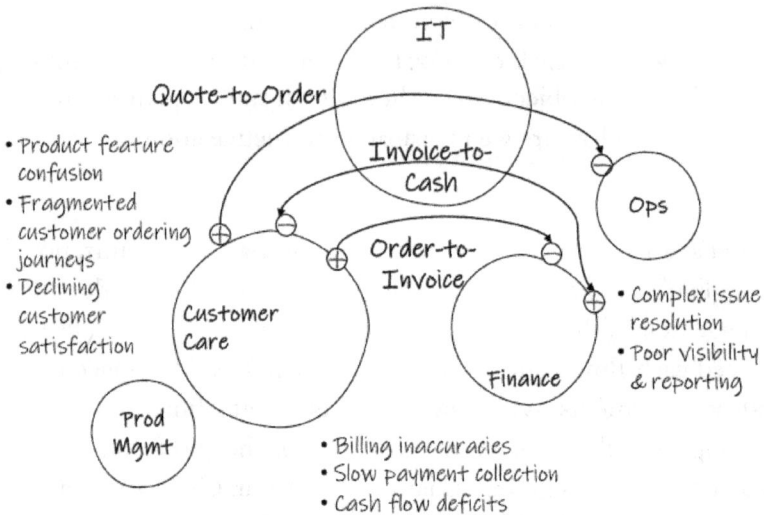

In addition to the issues brought to the table by the finance team, other organizations weighed in on their challenges as well. Customer care is struggling with their vast product catalog and customer profiles, as well as a growing customer dissatisfaction with their buying experiences. The operations team reports a general malaise around constant scrambling and firefighting just to get orders out the door.

After the first session, the CTO shared a coffee-urn observation with the other ELT members: "Did you notice that no one was calling out members of other teams by their functional roles? It was always *finance* or *ops* are doing this or that. I don't think the left hand knows that it even has a right hand, let alone what it's doing." The workshop group is asked to add an interim session in the agenda to peel back a layer on the organizational onion to make sure that everyone is aware of orchestration needed to turn an order into cash and how everyone at the table is positioned to make that happen (Figure 9).

Figure 9. Order-to-Cash Functional Teams

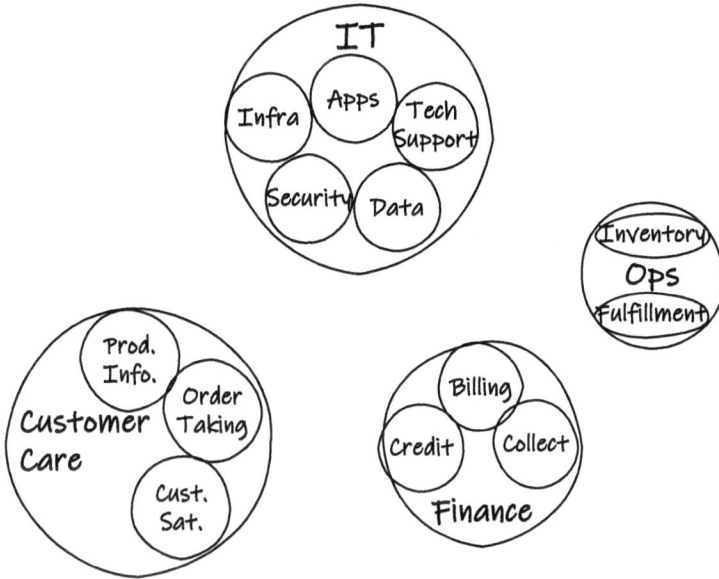

As each functional team member describes their role, it also becomes clear that not only do they take issue with the way the order-to-cash (or O2C) process is running, but that they are struggling to get their arms around it, in part, because they have enough issues to manage *within* their organization. The IT team members described three huge projects to consolidate their data centers to streamline their operations while experimenting with a "bi-modal" innovation model in support of new product introductions and re-factoring their legacy code for greater agility. Similar intraorganizational tensions were shared, and so the group took to whiteboarding it (Figure 10).

Figure 10. Intraorganizational Tensions

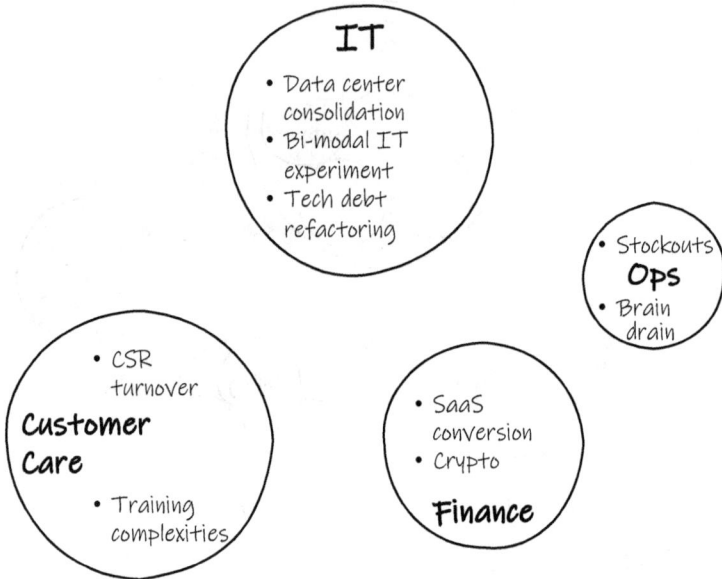

With full accountability and transparency on the walls, the group began to map all the tensions that they observed between their organizations across the O2C process, where things fell down, misaligned strategic intent, where they felt resistance to resolving issues, and gaps in resources to make change. The walls were now covered in multi-colored marker ink, sticky notes, and raw emotion.

During their lunch break, the workshop facilitator took the initiative to summarize what they saw as the formidable challenges to take forward (Figure 11):

1. Shadow IT: work orders languish in IT queues, so customer care buys and installs software tools outside the approved process

2. Failure to communicate: operations overloads IT with reporting requests, so IT sets up a "portal" with layers of approvals and prioritizations

3. Policy shopping: since each payment method (credit card, crypto, gift cards, etc.) runs through a separate system, CSRs encourage customers to pay only via credit cards
4. Passive-aggressive adoption of the new ERP system

Figure 11. Interorganizational Tensions

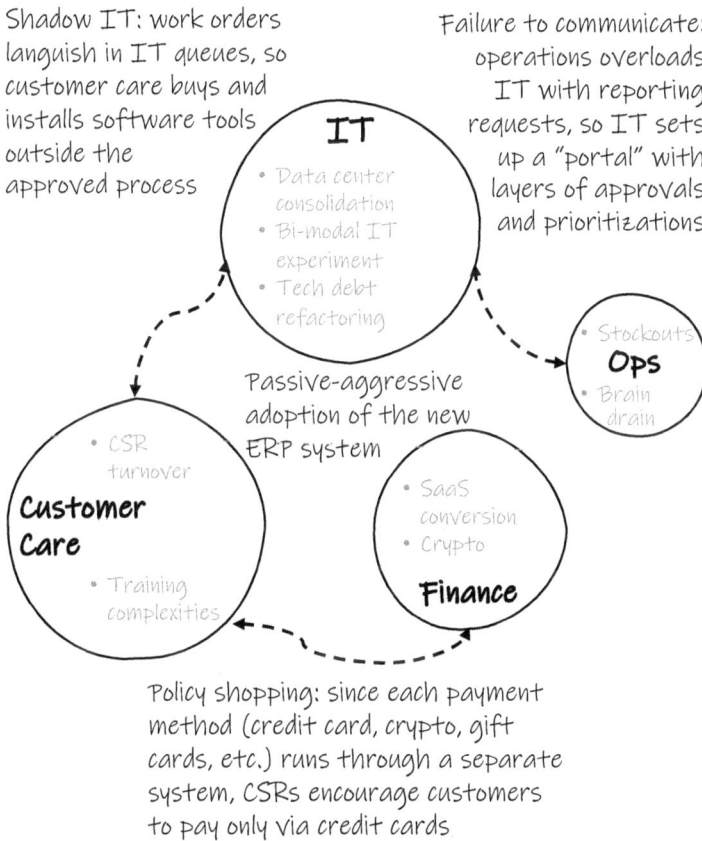

Shadow IT: work orders languish in IT queues, so customer care buys and installs software tools outside the approved process

Failure to communicate: operations overloads IT with reporting requests, so IT sets up a "portal" with layers of approvals and prioritizations

IT
• Data center consolidation
• Bi-modal IT experiment
• Tech debt refactoring

Ops
• Stockouts
• Brain drain

Passive-aggressive adoption of the new ERP system

Customer Care
• CSR turnover
• Training complexities

Finance
• SaaS conversion
• Crypto

Policy shopping: since each payment method (credit card, crypto, gift cards, etc.) runs through a separate system, CSRs encourage customers to pay only via credit cards

With the tension mapping on the wall, the facilitator sensed some mixed feelings in the room. They believed each team member was at the same time nodding in agreement to the tensions relating to other teams, but not entirely convinced about the assessment where it hit home. The facilitator asked for more tangible artifacts to back up claims of tension. "We're gonna need to bring the receipts," they declared. The group was given an extended coffee break so they could dig up documentation of their observations and interorganizational dilemmas. Those artifacts were posted on the walls (Figure 12), with some time allotted for the team members involved to authenticate and talk through a bit.

Figure 12. Tension Fact-Checking

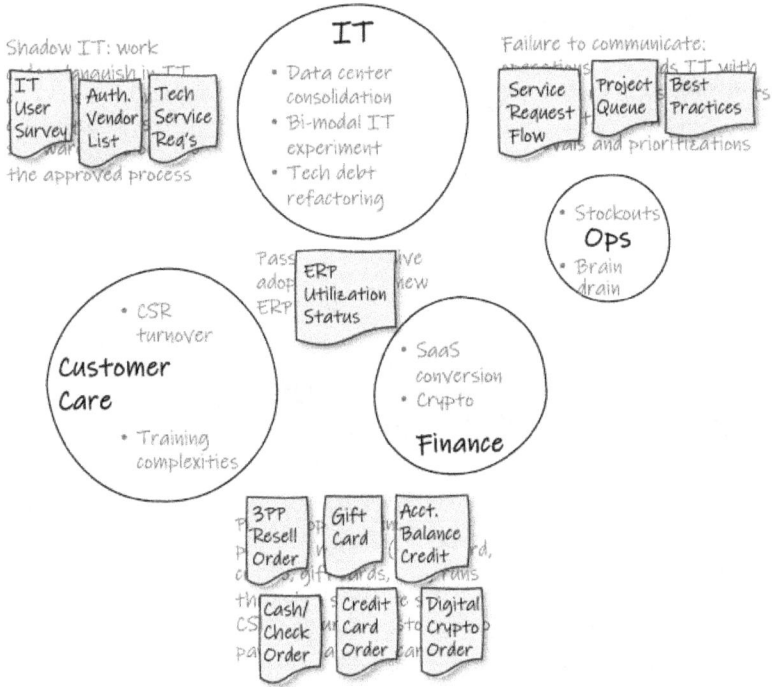

After surveying the seemingly disparate policy and protocol documentation, an operations team member raised a concern from the workshop objectives whiteboard that their interorganizational objectives might be misaligned or suboptimized, cascading into a seemingly fragmented end-to-end process. As the group dug up

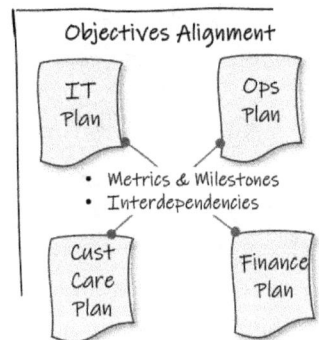

their individual plans, metrics, and milestones, they asked the CFO for clarification on how metrics were meant to be aligned and how milestone dependencies across organizations were aligned.

The CFO thoughtfully opined:

Today, we expect that our goals are only achievable through a distribution of work through the appropriate organizations. We are driven by an expectation of measurable performance. We distribute our corporate goals to each organization, empowering them to define their team objectives necessary to contribute to those goals. In reality, that's where our oversight ends. We, unfortunately, don't manage whether those teams truly believe in the corporate goals or view them as achievable. We also don't have a resolution process when interdependencies turn into what we dub in the finance org as "milestone chicken," where one team doesn't have faith that the other will meet their interdependent milestone, and they create workarounds or appropriate tasks to keep a project on schedule.

Through the lens of intentional tension, we need to redesign our O2C process with enough productive tension that we push collectively toward our goals while alleviating the impediments to the production of outcomes, or negative tensions, that come from unstructured competition of resources or lack of participation in a shared objective. We need a banner above our whiteboards here that reads "I support you in that."

With what appears to be all their cards on the table, the group decides they are ready to advance into the Tension Balancing session. To mix up the dynamic, they also decide to split up into the break-out rooms to dig into the root causes for the tensions displayed throughout the conference room. The thinking was that such a large group would risk "consensus thinking," where what they really wanted was something much more abstract or conjectured even... completely original ways of looking at their obstacles.

After the breakouts, the group reconvened, taking turns at a blank whiteboard to fill out a root cause artifact (Figure 13).

Figure 13. Tension Sources & Root Causes

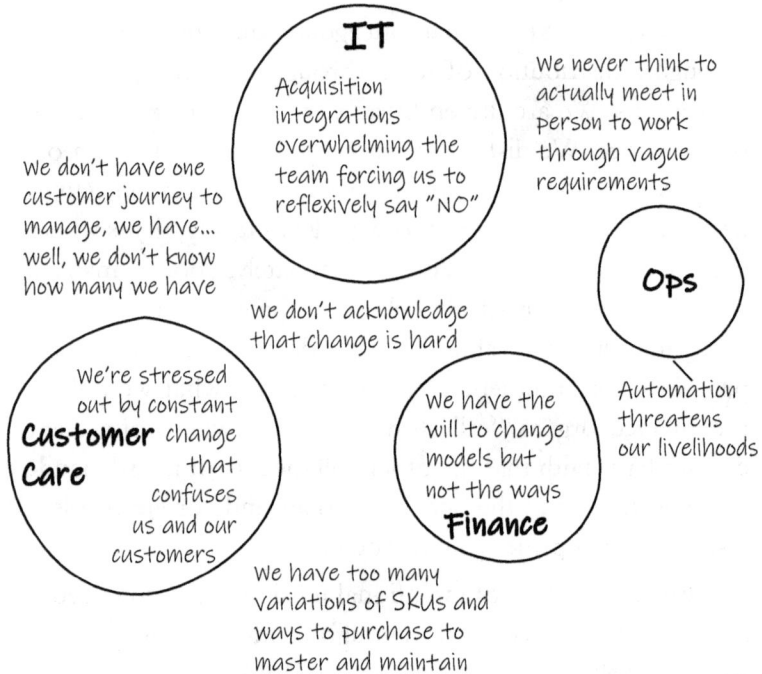

The group was pleased that they had unearthed the sources of tension, down to the ways they thought and felt about their work, their fears and stubbornness, and a recognition that structural issues were undermining trust throughout the O2C process. They felt ready to tackle those structural issues, with full confidence that the intentional tension perspective would keep them from slipping into the *technology panaceas* that they had cautioned themselves against at the outset of the meeting. The IT team did, however, take the pen for the next exercise of turning the intentional tensions mapping into a rational, managed structural transformation (Figure 14).

Figure 14. Intentional Tension Mapping: O2C Process

How might we:
- Enable us to delight the customer
- Enable us to manage the business performance
- Enable us to provide valuable, integrated solutions

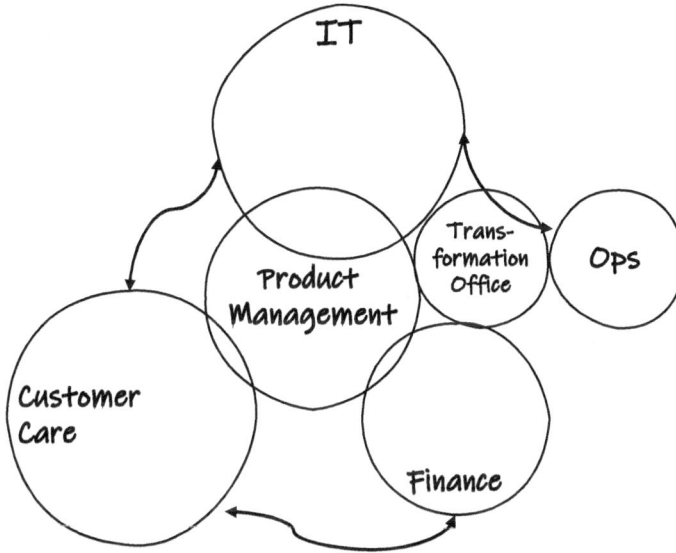

Systemic rethinking:
- Pull in product management to provide teams with ROI-driven requirements, customer journeys, user story priorities, and roadmaps
- Create a transformation office to address technology innovation, post-merger integration, and business model resourcing, skilling, and communication
- Redesign and fund a streamlined system estate focused on accuracy and speed

They started by leading a discussion of how they might systematically rethink the O2C process to optimize the tensions end to end. After much iteration and crumpled up ideas that ended up in the waste basket, they landed on a set of clean and clear desired outcomes.

The executive leaders were truly amazed by the out-of-the-box thinking they were witnessing, including the recommendation to bring the product management function into the O2C fold and for the ELT to consider creating a new transformation office as a sandbox for enterprise innovation and change. From there, the IT team worked their magic at the whiteboard to illustrate their legacy O2C architecture that had been built over many years and how they might redesign their system estate to support the intentional tension objectives, starting with the current estates (Figure 15).

Figure 15. Order-to-Cash Current State

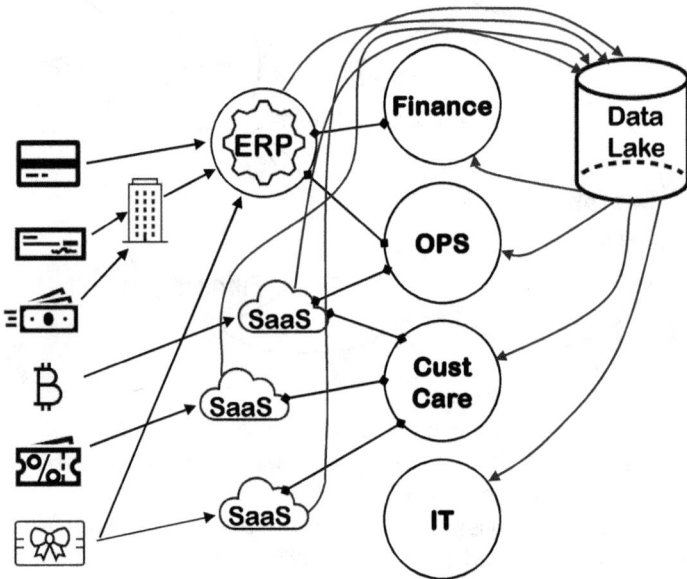

The IT team then led a surprisingly interactive discussion with the group about what a redesigned system estate might look like. They were surprised in that they had never experienced such participation with their peers from other organizations on requirements, desired outcomes, potential unintended consequences, and risk mitigation. The workshop group landed on a new system estate plan that they could all support and fund willingly (Figure 16).

Figure 16. O2C Redesigned System Estate

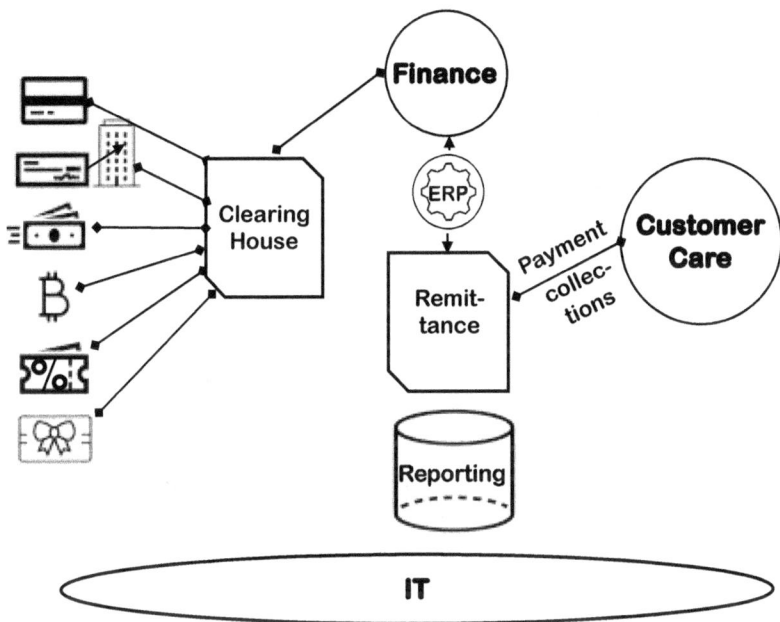

At this point, the group took the added step of expanding the tension map to other organizations that might be impacted in lesser ways by the revised O2C process. The CTO invited in the head of internal communications to help socialize the changes across the company. Sales and marketing working groups would also be assembled in the coming days to create a communications plan to share any value adds with customers and partners. HR and training teams were asked to ponder the automation and reskilling concerns. An informal O2C task force emerged from volunteers from the workshop who would meet regularly with the larger stakeholder group and periodically report on the progress of the tension map to the ELT.

In this chapter, we have also begun to identify the first layer of our Intentional Tension Model:
- o   Have a plan and execute
- o   Know how work is done
- o   Operate in the open
- o   Tune the racket

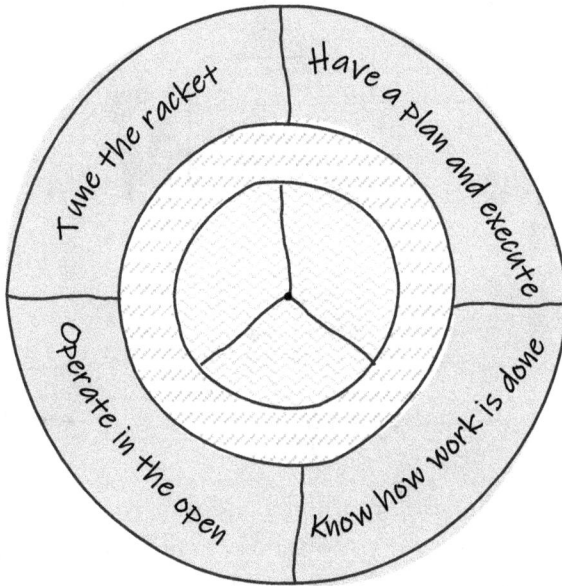

Next, we will turn our attention to the ultimate use case of intentional tensions... one that most, if not all of us, have or will experience at some point in our careers. Mergers & Acquisitions! We wanted to write an entire book on the subject, but after deep consultation with the colleagues on our dedication page, the views and insights on M&A and post-merger integration were so diverse that we could write two volumes just on the strategies and challenges. What was clear and inescapable in their stories was the pervasive and problematic organizational tensions that undermined the intended value creation and growth.

4

ACQUISITIONS—THE PERFECT STORM OF TENSION

There are no Mergers, only Acquisitions! There really is no such thing as a merger: In an M&A transaction, one company acquires the other. Acquisition is a widely used practice to grow one's business. However, great care and caution must be taken to ensure the maximal chance of success, as many acquisitions fail to meet their intended business and financial goals in one way or another... When one company decides to buy another, what happens next is one part financial and legal execution and one part alchemy.

There are no Mergers, only Acquisitions!

With all their hopes and expectations in mind, the leadership team makes a series of critical decisions, hopefully with significant consideration and intent. The most vital and immediate choice is how the acquired company will be organized within the acquiring company. The acquired company may be made to feel like they have a say in the post-merger integration outcomes, but the power lies fully with the ones taking the risk and making the investment.

There really is no one-size-fits-all, but our best advice is to strike a balance between full and no integration and get it done quickly. Integration decisions are best implemented within the first 100 days post-close. This allows the teams to get past the emotions, move on to implementing the agreed-upon structure, and start to execute together.

Why? Let's look back to our analogy of the tennis racket. Think about the tension map of your own company the last time you made an acquisition. How is it constructed, and what are the key sources of positive and negative tension (potential energy)? Sales has its objectives already. Marketing has a fixed budget for the year, and this deal is likely not calculated into their plans. Engineering has a set of standards, and regardless of recent improvements in cloud technology, any two companies involved in a "merger" have undoubtedly made vastly different choices in their application and development of technology. Years of product development and IT architecture decisions have contributed to vast technology estates that are painful to manage standalone and, moreso, to rationalize and integrate.

Now, for a moment, think about the company that has just been acquired. What does their tension map look like? Maybe they are significantly smaller, with much of the energy that drives the company coming from a founder or a set of principals who built it from the ground up. In these types of companies, the tension map looks like a few people pulling and pushing on all aspects of the company to drive its daily execution.

Or, on the contrary, think about the tension map of a much larger company than the one being acquired after failing to deliver on its strategic objectives. The acquisition was preceded by a very complex mesh of existing tensions between organizations, people, and reward systems. These types of companies have another unseen force as well: *organizational inertia*. You will know it when you see and hear it. Organizational inertia sounds like, "This is the way we do things," or "We tried it a different way before and it failed, so we do it this way," or "This is just our culture." Culture is a real and powerful force in a company, but it is also owned by no one and can be a proxy for every sort of resistance to change. More on that later, but first, let's step back and look at how acquisitions can so quickly nosedive from good intentions to a tempest of tensions.

It has been said by colleagues of ours that the only reason a company would buy another and then eliminate its leadership team is that the acquirer believes they are smarter and have more insight than the current leaders.

The only reason a company would buy another and then eliminate its leadership team is that the acquirer believes they are smarter and have more insight than the current leaders.

In one example of merger tensions at the leadership level, we once worked for a great company that had gone through its fair share of growth, contraction, and growth again. The company had replaced its entire leadership team save a few select people about two years before COVID-19 hit. The new leadership team had a plan, was tight-knit, and executing. So much so that the company had hit bottom and turned to growth within the first six months of its turnaround. The CEO was simply outstanding, full of industry knowledge, sound business judgment, and literally one of the best people leaders we had ever worked for. These were days of excellence. Yeah, there were tensions in the organizations and between them, but they were managed. If ever one party started to introduce negativity and unproductive force upon the business, the leaders would meet, strike a compromise, and quickly return the business to balance. If there was a needed stretch for a new customer opportunity, sure, we would fight it out for a while, but always within the frame of mutual goals and objectives and, frankly, respect for one another.

Let us take you back to the beginning of the pandemic. We just did not know what was going to happen next. Some people believed that the world would forever be changed, travel would never resume at the same level as before, social gathering would not pick back up, and the end of society was upon us all. We would all be-come even more insular, disconnected, and disengaged physically, and, as a result, the products and services of this company would no longer be needed. The board of directors faced a very difficult set of decisions, given their role to protect and increase shareholder value.

Others believed that the whole thing would just blow over, the world would quickly get back to business, and therefore, our op-portunity was delayed but not eliminated. This camp was about right-sizing the workforce to preserve the essential value of the en-terprise until sunny days would eventually return. As leaders and employees, we did our best, frankly, to maintain calm and continue to execute as the leadership team met with the board to determine the plan for the enterprise.

Eventually, it was decided that the company would be sold to an interested competitor. This company was very well known to us all and very much focused on low-cost leadership. They were smaller but very strong executors who favored the advantages of scale and commoditization over our legacy of leading with creativ-ity and customization. The mechanics of the deal were efficient and quick, and our company was in play within weeks of the board's decision to sell. The normal process ensued with due diligence, economic analysis, and ultimately, meetings with both of our lead-ership teams. The acquiring company's leadership was likewise very tight and focused but more so on the combined economics for their business than the people or culture we had built. Although they would not share their plans for a post-integration company structure, it was very evident that they would select the lowest-cost option over all others. Many meetings took place where the unspo-ken truth came more and more to the forefront. They had a technology estate and were comfortable with it, although they fully recognized its feature/function was less than ours. It was good enough. They had an office environment and were likewise satis-fied. Their customers were used to receiving value in a specific manner, and they were convinced that our customers would just adapt to their model as well.

So, what was the need for the executive team of our acquired company? There was none, in the acquiring leadership team's view. All the happy talk was over, and we were all to meet with them one by one, face to face if possible (a challenge during the pandemic). Each of them did so, and the meetings sounded all the same: "We appreciate the sale of your business, but your services will not be needed going forward." This was the case across the board, with the exception of a few executives who were asked to consult during the transition.

Adan as the acquired company's CTO expressed: Everyone needs technology transformation, so his management conversation was a bit different and about a future of total integration and optimization and, frankly, elimination of much of the work his team had done. The discussion was about the near-total elimination of their technology projects, innovation projects, and most of the people. Under these constraints, he was given the opportunity to remain in his post. To this, he simply laid down his pencil, so to speak, and asked to exit with his peers on the same dates and terms, and this is what was done.

Most of Adan's team was quickly eliminated, and the acquirer followed through on the full integration. This was an example of total integration and the total elimination of the culture and leadership of the acquired company. Was it successful? Given the industry and the scale of operations of the combined company, probably yes, on the basis of the economics alone. Was it as successful as it could have been? No one will ever know, but our feeling is that a lot of potential value was lost. There was no thought given to, or discussion about, how to weave the companies together in a manner that would maximize their productive force. There was no consideration beyond minimizing the cost per unit of work. The company and its people were merely additional costs to be managed, and manage those costs is what they did.

We admire their dedication to their business strategy but lament the loss of the acquired innovation, not to mention the impact on the people during a time of great worldwide uncertainty.

Post-Merger Integration as a Tension Force Multiplier

Acquisitions seem to play out more like the television series *Survivor* than a quest for synergies and shareholder value. The sources of merger tensions are pervasive, starting with the merger strategy or lack thereof, haphazard reorganization tactics, and poor communications throughout. Here is just a sample of tension generators to which anyone who has experienced a merger can likely attest:

- We bought you, so *we* are in charge.
- You should be happy that we're even letting you interview for your job.
- The old leadership team are idiots! Why did you do it that way? Why did you not do it this way?
- Send me a one-page justification for keeping you in your current job.
- There have been no decisions made on the new organization—*yeah, right!* That's what you told everyone at the last three companies that you bought.
- Putting client needs last.
- Assuming competitors will sit idly by during your protracted integration.

Organizational antibodies

Organizational antibodies are hidden everywhere post-merger, but often, they were formed as the deal was conceived or before the deal was closed. In the classic "build versus buy" scenario, R&D leadership may have felt spited by the executive leadership's decision to acquire a capability rather than trying to build it in-house. It may have been perceived as a vote of no-confidence in the ability of the development team to bring a successful product to market faster and more effectively than some startup company.

The stage, therefore, is now set post-merger for stonewalling and an unspoken hope that their new teammates will fail.

Think about this statement for a moment. *Hoping to see the team fail!* Unfortunately, this is all too common and more the norm than the exception. This is clearly not the hope or expectation of the principals who conceived of the acquisition. They were hoping for collaboration and value creation. But, as we have said, "Hope is not a plan."

In anticipation of such defensiveness, the acquiring company's leadership may decide to isolate the new asset from attack by separating the new team in a standalone organization. Without the full support of marketing, sales, and operations, the subject matter experts in the new entity leave, and the intellectual property dissipates with the brain drain, as no knowledge transfer was allowed to incur.

Acquisitions create tensions not just at the organizational level but also at the human level. People feel like *the rug was pulled out from under them.* They liked the work they were doing, they had career paths in front of them in a young and growing organization, and they worked hard to establish their reputation with the leadership of that company. Now that the leadership team is gone, the direction of the new company is unclear, and they are interviewing for their jobs. The tensions appear suddenly and are everywhere.

Even when the management teams on both sides want to make things work, the lack of strategic leadership intent creates tension chaos. In some cases, the board or executive leadership may have made the decision to make the acquisition without consulting the unit management teams. It may have been opportunistic—where an investment bank approached them with a financially-driven takeover opportunity—or secretive so as not to inflate the share price of the target.

Once the deal is done, the leadership team drops the new asset into the laps of their management team and moves on. The strategic intent may not be clearly documented, promises may have been made to the leadership of the target to get the deal done that were

POPE AND BUONFIGLIO

not conveyed to others in the organization, and the expectations for synergies were not fully vetted.

The sounds of such tensions usually manifest themselves in disbelief:

- o "How could you possibly sell the value of this business without including me? I've been in this industry for almost 20 years!"
- o "How could they possibly understand the value of what they purchased?"
- o "How could they understand the operational complexity associated with this business?"
- o "For our technology to not be mentioned as the critical aspect of how the business is valued is just wrong and nonsensical!"
- o "They said that execution was one of their core values, but then they vanished after the sugar rush of the transaction wore off!"

Let's look now at a hypothetical acquisition, given our newly acquired perspective on tension. Can we use the lens of tension to create the impossible—an actual *merger*?

Acquisition as a Stress Test of Tension Mapping

As leaders, we must always be mindful of the tensions in our company and organizations. The goal is not only to be mindful but also to be intentional. To be intentional implies that we understand the way work gets done, the process of the business, and the people dynamics that are in play. Leadership is truly an art of action based on knowledge and empathy. As in physics, every action has a reaction and consequence—and every non-action has a consequence as well.

BigCo and SmallCo

To illustrate the key concepts of intentional tension management mapping, consider the fictional case of SmallCo and BigCo. SmallCo is a company in the south of Ireland. The company started out doing what a lot of bootstrap start-ups do. They seek projects where they can apply their skills to solve and deliver while making enough money to pay their team and form the seed of a company. The founders are a bunch of engineers who place no limits on their ambition, scope, scale, or type of problems they choose to solve. They have some familiarity with telecommunications and industrial goods processing, so they start looking into those segments for project work. Fortunately, one of them is also a highly articulate sales professional and is able to convince their first telecommunications customer to take them on to solve a key problem the company is having related to the management of their assets during the rollout of a complex new service.

Off to an amazing start, they are able to move from one project to the next over the course of a few years and grow to a scale of 50 engineers and 20 million euros in annual revenues. Due to all of their great work, their reputation for delivery and excellence is solid, with one hundred percent referenceability with all customers. Play it forward a few more years, and SmallCo has a product now that truly solves the general problems they learned about during their initial founding. They take on outside investments, and rightfully, their investors see an opportunity for growth from the pivot of a skilled software solutions company to that of a software product company.

SmallCo formed, grew, sought investment to grow more, made a decision to become a product company, and is in search of more predictable and sustainable growth.

The SmallCo team is tight knit; they know one another, they trust one another, the organization is very flat, and there is no patience for anything but excellence. They practically live together, there is high admiration for the leadership, and the employees act as if they were family. Everyone has a potential financial stake in the growth of the business, and you can feel the energy of the place when you are at their location or even on a video call.

When they started out, the structure was extremely loose and consisted of three founders equally sharing the leadership of the company. All three leaders also did the work of the company, and over time, one of them became head of engineering, one took on head of sales, and the other became head of services and support. When they started, work got done as follows: win a deal, do work, deliver to the customer, repeat. As they took on new investment, one of the investors joined as CEO, and the three leaders reported to him (Figure 17). The culture did not shift as the investor was viewed as having a real stake in not only the profits of the company but also its daily operations and fit in quickly with their can-do egalitarian culture.

Figure 17. SmallCo Professional Services & Single Product

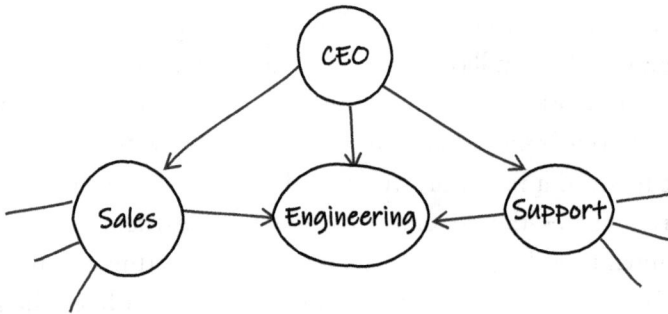

As time went on, SmallCo began to focus more and more of its energy and investment on its product platform. The original customers were migrated to their platform, and SmallCo needed to now become a scale product company or a services company with a product. The choice to focus on products was the reason for the investment, so this was the direction the company pursued. But in order to make this pivot, they needed to invent new products and sign up partners for their products.

Having a start like SmallCo, with the success that followed, is very rare. So many companies like SmallCo fail early on or become lifestyle businesses for their founders that just exist to pay the wages of a few people rather than create sustainable growth.

SmallCo started as a professional services company and then created one product. Many of the people working for SmallCo started to question the multiproduct strategy and advocated for a return to services as the best way to continue to be successful. How could they just invent new products? They had only done so through intensive iteration with customers. The investors were not in favor of this conservative approach and steered the company ahead toward a multiproduct strategy. But how?

Stepping out from our story for a moment, can you feel the tensions rising from this strategic pivot? The things that had made it successful, while valuable, were no longer sufficient to fuel their growth expectation. When they were starting out, every deal was vital, incremental growth. Customers were happy because they delivered whatever the customer asked for. The structure was fluid, and the founders all made the call about priorities and approaches to business.

Which means that...

The tensions of SmallCo were directly managed by the founders, who all shared the potent experience of winning together. A lack of clear structure did not hinder the company's growth. On the rare occasion that there was a problem between people, it got solved quickly, and the company moved on. No politics and no fear, except for the start-up fear of extinction, of course.

Now that the company had committed to a multiproduct strategy, how were they going to be able to execute? How would they make the right bets while not risking the success they have attained thus far?

The first thing they did was to offer their product as a service. In order to do so, they created a technical operations team that reported to engineering. While this did grow the revenue of the business and create a repeatable cash flow, SmallCo still only had one product which was now offered as a service. SmallCo then invested in the development of a research team and the creation of a very thin product management organization.

The mission of these teams was to learn the needs of their customers, identify opportunities for adjacent offers, and create innovative products that SmallCo customers would be willing to buy in conjunction with their current core product. The move to the XaaS (every product or every product category offered as a service) service model alone created the demand for additional employees, and the business grew to a scale where it needed a human resources function. Further, SmallCo now had taken on enough investment money and new customers that they required a finance function to keep track of it all and make sure they were compliant with all of their investor obligations. With time, persistence, and some luck, SmallCo was able to become a product company with five products in its portfolio, all of which were offered either on premises via licensed software sale or as a service. SmallCo is still a small company, but it has met the challenge of growth and scale.

The way work gets done now at SmallCo (Figure 18) is based on a sophisticated tension map between all of its organizations. Each organization has a leader, a set of objectives, and dependencies on their related organizations. In the good old days, work was sold and then delivered by many of the same people. Now, product management and sales seek to understand the needs and challenges of the company's potential customers. Sales also has to bring in the bookings for the year, so their incentives are not exactly aligned to the need for long-term growth, but the tension is managed via sales incentives for lead customers.

Research determines the key requirements and must-have capabilities of new products that could serve the identified potential need, as well as offering all sorts of concepts for sales and product management to pitch. In some cases, a prototype is made and then iterated with high-potential early-adopter customers. Then, engineering takes on the task of developing the new product that meets current requirements and also has intentional design flexibility for future iterations and scale should the product take off in the market. Production support ramps up and builds processes and automation to deploy and scale the products for customers' use, and the customer and service organization ready training and support services.

Figure 18. Tension Stakeholders of SmallCo Multi-Product

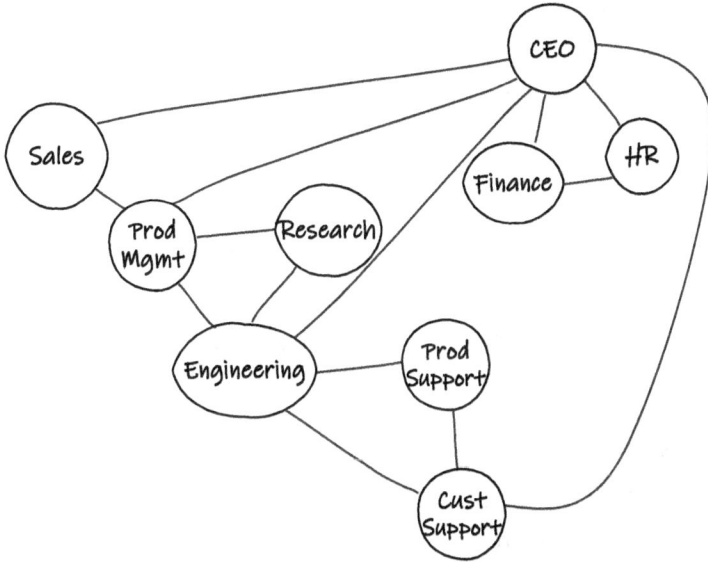

While all this is happening, real money is being invested in people—as the company grows, so do the needs of SmallCo employees. Competitors are circling and looking to poach key talent. A head of human resources has been hired to ensure that employee compensation and benefits are in line with the market and that the culture is in alignment with the leaders and board. The board and the CEO also seek to balance the risk and reward of these investments, so the financial rigor of the company increases to ensure that investments are rational and risk-adjusted; as such, a CFO has been hired to help the company invest in growth and balance returns.

SmallCo has really undergone a lot of transformation and growth, but at its core still is SmallCo, just with new players, success, and additional scale. The tensions of the company can no longer be intentionally managed by the founders as many new investors, leaders, entire organizations, and employees have joined, all bringing with them their experiences and expectations. As the increase in scale drives an increase in complexity, the sense of direct ownership and accountability declines, but the culture holds true to form.

Which means that…

The leaders of SmallCo, while successful in growing the business to this stage, have an even greater need to look carefully at the way work is done now. This would be challenging as all the history has no doubt created an operating *shorthand* that may no longer hold true. The leaders now establish a set of company-wide objectives, tasking the functional leaders with creating their own objectives in direct alignment. Above all else, they know they must stay true to their leadership principles [as adopted from *Respect the Weeds*, Part III: Putting the Plan into Action] focused on accountability, transparency, empathy, and humility. That, combined with the formidable success and ambition of SmallCo, serves as the root of its culture.

As we park the story of SmallCo, hopefully, you get the sense of the way work gets done and accountability is taken. SmallCo is a highly entrepreneurial start-up that is proud of its history and full of employees who collaborate freely, creating and relieving tension for the best outcomes of their business and its customers. SmallCo is not very corporate. It's all about the people and the way they work together that makes SmallCo successful and magical in its own way.

The Story of BigCo

BigCo was founded over 100 years ago and has become the de facto standard bearer of its industry. Over the long and impressive span of operations, BigCo has developed a very scalable and highly standardized approach to its product development, support, and regional sales and service execution.

Products are developed in centralized product business units. BigCo has many product business units that all operate on the same principles and methodology. Further, BigCo has a central strategy and planning function, which is chartered with consolidating all product business units' business and technology plans, reviewing them, approving or rejecting them, and, in many cases, guiding them toward a set of corporate strategic imperatives set by the board. Everything BigCo does is fashioned to scale development operations and sales execution.

This regimented approach works well, except that the growth rate for BigCo has slowed dramatically over the past few years, even as they strive for innovation and product diversification. They have tried to mandate innovation to the product business units but have only been able to achieve incrementalism within the constraints of the product business unit charters.

A series of rules has developed over the years to keep order within the scale of the business. For example, product business units are not required to collaborate and must stand on their own in terms of accountability and results. Each product business unit, though, follows the corporate strategic mandates as well as their roadmap based on the market research relevant to their industry segment.

Further, region-specific operational units are only allowed to sell products that come from the product business units, and they must negotiate with the product business units on commercial terms if they are outside of corporate standards. Technology innovation ideas are welcomed by all participants and ultimately decided on by the product business unit or the centralized strategy function of the business.

Within the organizational design of BigCo (Figure 19), the functions within each area are highly standardized and tuned for scale. This high degree of standardization has made it common for employees and leaders to move freely between regions and product business units. Standardization and compliance with the corporate strategy are prized more than subject matter expertise or individualism.

Figure 19. BigCo Organizational View

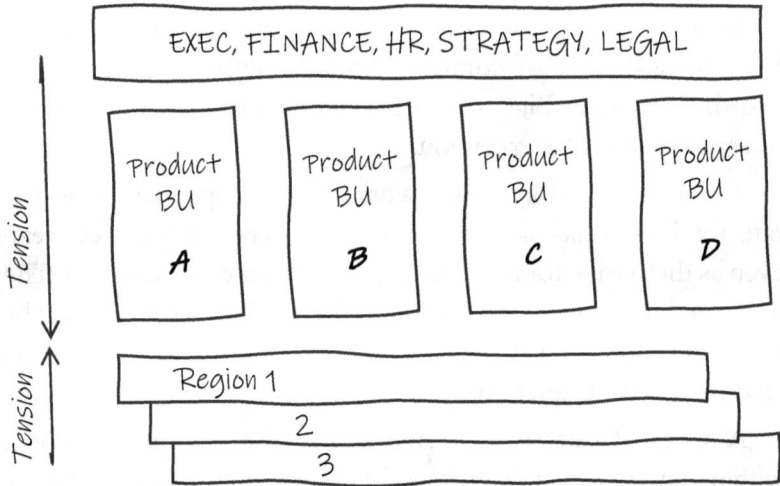

Which means that to have a successful career in BigCo, one needs to be committed to the standard processes of BigCo and be willing to move freely between the product business units and regions. Employees effectively become "citizens" of BigCo, and it is quite common for people to work their entire professional career for BigCo and retire as alumni.

BigCo Acquires SmallCo

The corporate strategy team of BigCo has formulated an investment thesis to enter the core product business where SmallCo has its products and customers. The board of SmallCo has been offered a deal to sell SmallCo to BigCo in an all-cash transaction that results in the achievement of the desired returns for SmallCo's investors, so the sale is agreed upon and finalized. *Now what?*

After all the requisite due diligence is performed and the money exchanges hands, the employees of SmallCo are now employed by BigCo. Beyond the significant differences in scale and space, the sheer difference in workflow within SmallCo and that of a large multinational company like BigCo is stark. In BigCo, they do everything the same way regardless of the product business unit. They have invested in a way of working, and that way has served them well. They have likewise invested in acquiring the operations of SmallCo, and they expect them to respect their legacy of success. Simply put, BigCo is in charge of what happens next.

BigCo is now faced with the challenge of how to integrate SmallCo into the business. BigCo could just move SmallCo into its own product business unit structure, but SmallCo was a self-contained business possessing all the functions of an independent business. BigCo sketches out a potential organization assignment for SmallCo (Figure 20), integrating them into the BigCo standard operating model.

Figure 20. SmallCo as a Product Business Unit of BigCo

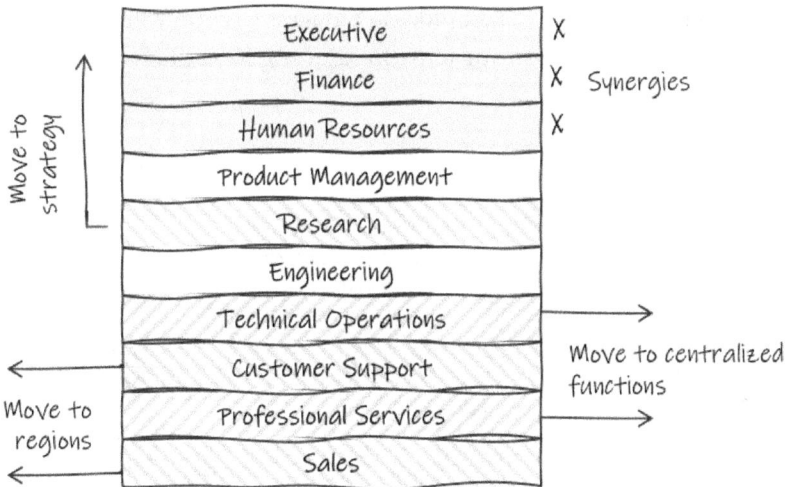

Clearly, this organizational integration strategy would destroy all sources of positive tension within SmallCo. SmallCo derives so much of its sense of purpose from its expertise, which has been developed through years of intimate customer interaction and understanding. The employees of SmallCo are experts in the business of SmallCo and have tremendous pride in their start-up to growth journey.

In addition to the shock this type of integration would have on SmallCo's employees, the organizations within BigCo where they would be moved would likely have no experience with the markets SmallCo serves nor the operational expense in their budgets or sales mandates in their plans for the first year of the transaction.

We won't go too much further into the best organizational integration strategy for BigCo and SmallCo except to state the obvious: Applying BigCo's standard post-acquisition integration approach would destroy SmallCo and create so much negative tension that it would be surprising if many people from SmallCo remained within BigCo for very long.

From what we learned in Chapter 3, take a moment to think about what the tension map might look like in this scenario (Figure 21). What other tensions would you envision? If you were the CEO of BigCo, what would your tension *sweet spot* look like?

Figure 21. Pre-Integration Tension Planning

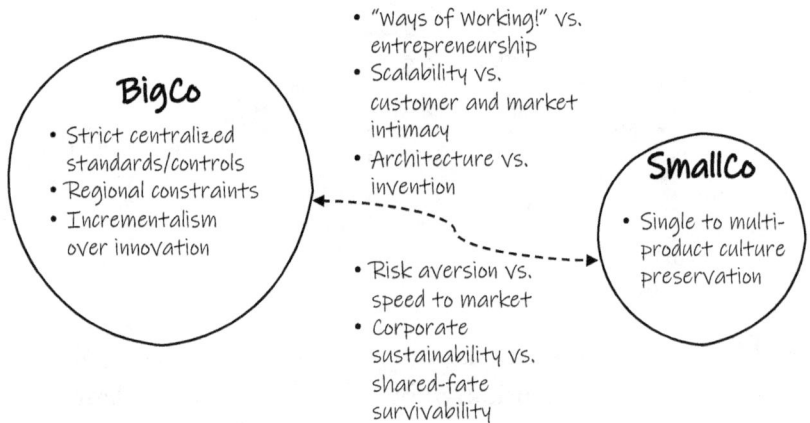

BigCo
- Strict centralized standards/controls
- Regional constraints
- Incrementalism over innovation

- "Ways of Working!" vs. entrepreneurship
- Scalability vs. customer and market intimacy
- Architecture vs. invention
- Risk aversion vs. speed to market
- Corporate sustainability vs. shared-fate survivability

SmallCo
- Single to multi-product culture preservation

SmallCo was purchased for a reason. The investment thesis was authored by BigCo's strategy team with the express purpose of product and market expansion. No company purchases another to destroy the value they purchased. If BigCo can understand the systems of tension that drive the way work gets done within SmallCo and connect those to their corporate structure, leaving the core of SmallCo in place, they have a chance to gain the value they sought by bringing a proud but small company into their corporate portfolio.

Much success has been had incorporating small companies into larger ones by considering them incubators for a market. As the products of SmallCo become more widely adopted and deployed due to the scale of BigCo, SmallCo could transform into a proper, fully standard product business unit. Until then, it is best managed in an advised and guided manner (not subsumed), except for the incentives provided to BigCo's regional sales and operations teams. This, too, presents a number of challenges, and incentive programs need to be very thoughtfully designed. If a region believes that selling SmallCo amounts to nothing but risk with little or no reward, the outcome is predictable and won't be an accretive one.

Figure 22 illustrates a potential structure where SmallCo acts as a market incubator could look like within BigCo. This approach enables BigCo to allow SmallCo to incubate new market offers for BigCo. In this model, SmallCo needs to be protected as it will likely be viewed and measured against the BigCo standard unless special efforts are made to prevent this. We are not recommending that BigCo ignore SmallCo; instead, we recommend that BigCo nurture it and integrate it as the scaled-up demand becomes evident. At that point, SmallCo will have secured its portfolio relevance and found its place among the other product business units of BigCo.

The storyline of SmallCo and BigCo frequently takes place in one manner or another as businesses seek growth through acquisition. Our purpose in sharing this story is to encourage discussion about intentional tension management *prior to* the duress of an acquisition.

Figure 22. SmallCo Within BigCo Incubator

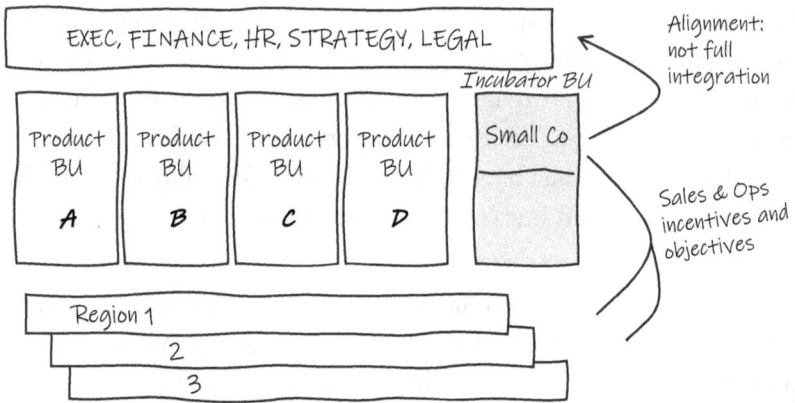

Acquisitions lead to tremendous stress and loss of productivity within the acquired company. Sometimes, this stress even infiltrates the acquirer if there is a widespread belief that integration will lead to layoffs based on "synergies" in the workforce. We encourage leaders to turn up their empathy as they consider their employees and the ways work gets done within both the acquired and the acquiring company. The individuals in both companies are coming together, likely not of their choosing. In order to create the desired growth, they must find a productive way to work within their new host company.

Which means that the leaders must be equipped with and willing to understand how work is done, the objectives and incentives of the newly combined company, and the tensions required and to be eliminated in order to improve the company's chances of success.

Intentional Tension as a Driver of Value Preservation

So, post-deal Day One is approaching, and it's time to start planning and executing the desired full integration of the acquired company. Where do you begin? Our advice? Get on with the easy stuff! Decide on the name of the company, if changing, its color palette, email addresses, and employee benefits. The integration team (or whoever has the authority to make such decisions) needs to convince the new organization to just accept it and move on! Otherwise, many hours will likely be spent trying to design an integrated logo and color palette that would only be a compromise for both companies and, in our experience, not worth the effort. Sorry to be so blunt, but some of this stuff really can and should be this easy. We accept that there will be many considerations to address in terms of legal entities, insurance brokers, etcetera, but common sense needs to rule these decisions—not a committee. The tension generators—who works for whom, what team leads an activity, and how people are compensated—are more difficult, worthy, and extremely important get-right decisions.

Think about weaving the acquired company's racket into the acquiring company, string by string and tension by tension. There are areas that require the parent organization to mesh with or drive the acquired company. For these, start with the people. Who are the leaders? Now that a new set of people has joined via the acquisition, you have the opportunity to choose from the combined resources of both companies. Given human nature and the fact that leaders really do matter in the integration and execution of the combined company, choose the best from the combined pool. It is generally a good idea to select some leaders from the acquired company over incumbents in the acquiring company so long as the approach is grounded in merit and the availability of skilled leaders. If you can take this approach, you will be signaling to the combined company that you value those who just joined as much as your existing staff.

Remember, the goal is to create more value, not destroy it. Buying a company and not taking stock of yourself or your newly acquired leadership team is likely short-sighted and compromises the opportunity for positive incorporation of the acquired within the acquiring party. It may sound obvious, but we need to start at the beginning if we are to improve the odds of achieving a successful acquisition.

Taking liberties with the scientific method, we might harness its power of systematic investigation to better understand complex problems and improve outcomes during the time of an acquisition and integration of a company. The search for a method from which to discern the truth of nature through observation, prediction, and evidence has been the fascination of scientists from the earliest records of formalized thought. In its simplest form, the (scientific method) approach might look like the following:

- o State your hypothesis
- o State the research
- o State the related theories
- o State the experiments that will be performed to either prove or disprove the hypothesis
- o Run the experiments and collect the data
- o Analyze the data
- o State the conclusions

This may sound a bit pedantic, formal, and rigorous when applied to the modeling of acquisitions… but that's exactly the point! It needs to be. If we cannot state clearly the outcomes we believe will occur and if we cannot link those outcomes to significant value creation for the business, then we have no basis to begin the treacherous journey of pursuing an acquisition.

With that in mind, let's restate the scientific method, modified to the value creation thesis for a business.

State what you expect to occur: What do you want to achieve in terms of growth rate and performance?

What specific results do you expect, and will you commit to for your business and its constituents from this acquisition? ("Growth in top-line revenue" is not a statement of strategy.) State your vision in terms of tangible outcomes you expect as a result of fulfilling the promises you will make to the market as this vision is executed.

For example: We aim to add scale to our current offer by x% [top line, bottom line, number of customers] and add breadth to our operations and portfolio by adding [widget 1, service 2, and partner 3] in region(s) X/Y/Z, thereby creating greater shareholder value by offering a broader range of products and/or services to our customers. Our larger scale will also enable us to serve the market at x% reduced cost (OPEX/CAPEX) through economies of scale created by realizing synergies from integrating the acquired company. In addition, we expect our employees will have enhanced career opportunities as we bring offer [1,2,3] online and go to market.

Take great care as you carefully think through, write, test, and rewrite what is desired from this acquisition before you make the decision to acquire. Whether you call it a wanted position or a value proposition, you need one, and it needs to be clear and convincing.

The value creation thesis forms the basis for the argument you will be making to the markets you participate in, the investors you may hope to attract, the customers you serve, and the people you employ.

The value creation thesis forms the basis for the argument you will be making to the markets you participate in, the investors you may hope to attract, the customers you serve, and the people you employ.

A clear argument starts with your vision, your belief in some future state, the features and benefits inherent in that future, and the measurements you intend to use to guide you and ensure progress along the way.

State your research: What market or competitive drivers exist?

In this step, you are seeking the information needed to determine who the competitors are, what analysts are following your industry, and what points of view are out there on the markets you serve. Also, what are the market segments and strategies you could exploit to achieve your goals?

This is an important step as it provides context and framing for your wanted position. When conducted thoroughly and honestly, this research lays the groundwork for realistically assessing your chances for success should the acquisition decision be made and executed.

For example, if your strategy is to acquire a product company that provides an application you believe will benefit your customers, then you need to have looked at the competition for this application, what you believe the market consolidation forces may be, and what effect (if any) your buying this company will have on the competitive landscape and your position within it.

State your related theories: How does the preferred approach to operating the business fit with the strategy you are pursuing?

Whatever we do to drive organic growth must fit within some context, initiative, and organization within the buying company (e.g., increase profitability or expand out of mature markets). The acquired business may be retained "intact" or "reverse integrated" or perhaps, most painfully, fully integrated into the acquiring company's existing structures. This choice is critical and fundamental to the success of any acquisition.

This step is valuable not only for assessing the strategy but also for providing the clarity critical for productive post-merger integration. Without adequate context for the acquisition, employees of both organizations (buyer and seller) will naturally try to "fill in the gaps" with their expected fears and anxieties, which will most certainly lead to a loss of momentum and productivity.

State the experiments you will perform to either prove or disprove your thesis.

Identify the metrics you will manage to and monitor that will serve as indicators of the success (or not) of the acquisition.

Many acquisitions we have been involved with suffered from a form of revisionist history. For example, in one case, the thesis was loosely written: "We aim to be #1 in the market for X product." But there were no viable measures for what it meant to be #1. We could measure profitable growth, number of new innovations, customer wins, market share, and more. Without this clarity and linkage to incentives, key players within the combined entity can become disenfranchised and leave the company; customers begin to lose faith; then, even if we ever could define #1, there was no way to achieve it. ("Work harder" or "sell more" is not a plan for success.)

As the adage goes, "You get what you measure." Some metrics are obvious, like market share and gross profit; while these are important and very tempting to focus on almost exclusively, they don't tell the full story about the progress of your acquisition or provide enough insight for course corrections. We need metrics across at least the following categories:

1) Objectives to achieve your strategy
2) Financial, profit, costs, synergies
3) People
4) Customers

These facets are connected to the strategic intent and value creation thesis. If you lose the people required to grow the business, then the financial opportunities may well slip away. Consider this "death spiral" scenario, one that we see all too often:

An incumbent market leader acquires a rival for their success in the hard-to-reach SMB (small and midsized business) market. To cover the premium they paid, they ask the retained leadership of the acquired company to improve their growth rates and EBITDA. During the post-merger integration planning, it was discovered that the operating expenses for the acquired company to service their SMB customers were higher than expected. In the search for "synergies," across-the-board cuts are made to their operating budgets, which leads to customer churn and lower growth. A new leadership team is installed from the legacy side of the acquirer, with limited SMB knowledge and experience, who try to deliver on operating margin targets with additional cost-cutting in lieu of informed investment or innovation. This fractures the culture that they needed to leverage in that elusive market.

Run the experiments and collect the data: Metrics

Collect data on the relevant metrics identified above and determine the appropriate cadence to do so. Initially, we recommend that you start with measuring what you can on the leading indicators for success of the acquisition frequently. Perhaps look at your employee retention data or acceptances of the retention plan (should you have one in place). You may also want to send a survey to employees to check the vibes and mood of the team.

While well-intentioned, the reality is that during a significant change initiative, such as an acquisition, many people simply will not answer out of fear, and those who do will expect to hear leadership follow up with a readout of what they learned and what they will do based on the input received. Surveys are fine, but a clear strategy, a clear value creation thesis, and an accompanying organization structure (one that is optimal across the business) will deliver on the value creation thesis more often than not.

Analyze the data and state your conclusions: Take action!

This step is critical in every industry and discipline. Measure, yes, but measurements or metrics that are not thoughtfully evaluated and considered when determining next steps are a waste of time. Also, for those doing the measurement, if we as leaders don't act on them, the company will begin either refusing to provide data or not trusting it.

Typically, a company might want its employees to embrace their post-merger market position. Leadership may ask to take the pulse of the staff as to whether they are *proud* of the company. Such a vague question is open to so much interpretation that only 20% of the employees respond (mostly those on the extreme ends of enthusiasm or disgruntlement). Not wanting to conflate that response to represent all of the company, a debate breaks among the leadership as to how "being proud" might have been interpreted and then whether it actually matters at all to the strategy of the company. Does a proud staff translate into competitiveness and continued market leadership?

Perhaps a more actionable approach might be to (1) ask the right questions, (2) make sure the data are as transparent and measurable as possible, and (3) create outcomes through data-informed actions (e.g., improve net promoter score by increasing product support for strategic offerings, offset by putting mature products in maintenance mode).

Write the press release as a test

An excellent way to test your value thesis is to write the acquisition press release *before* you enter into the exploration. This may sound like a trite exercise, but doing so forces you to think through the reasoning from the perspective of your numerous constituents. What strategy does the acquisition support? What are your motivations? What value will your shareholders gain? What value will your customers gain? What are the benefits for your employees?

While we may not have an equal distribution of benefits among stakeholders, it is imperative that we think through the impacts for each of them as they will draw their own conclusions if you don't address uncertainties through transparency.

Managing Uncertainty

News spreads throughout an acquired business like wildfire. Conversations between team members begin to take on an element of uncertainty and, potentially, anxiety or even fear that just was not there the day before the announcement. To compound this uncertainty, the time between the announcement of a deal and the actual change in control may be months long. This may lead to a real loss of productivity and general malaise settling into the operations of the soon-to-be-acquired company. For the acquiring company, there may well be a feeling of "hurry up and wait" due to the sense of urgency within the buyer colliding with a lack of ability to engage and execute with the acquired company and its employees.

The company you work for has been purchased. You have been assigned by the acquirer to work as a product management director in their new Enterprise Division, but they haven't identified a group leader for that division yet. You are still apparently responsible for the roadmaps for your product line, but you aren't provided a budget. How are you supposed to move a project forward? The doors to senior leadership are apparently closed, but you did get a directive to "hit all KPIs" (key performance indicators) during the transition. You're doomed.

Conspiracy theories start slowly but gain power quickly: *Maybe they are going to slash our budgets and outsource our jobs. Maybe they will shut down our office. Maybe they will stop the projects I've been working so hard on. Maybe I will be demoted. Maybe my new boss will be a micromanager and not a servant leader.* Fear is a terrible thing!

For employees of the acquired company, management needs them to carry on much as before the news. That is hard to do on day one and even harder each day that follows as a loss of faith in the control structures of the business and all the above fears take hold.

In our experience, in response to the uncertainty, leadership teams generally try to perpetuate a business-as-usual approach or try to take authoritarian control of the organization.

Business as usual (pretend nothing has changed)

This is typically what is desired by the leadership of both the buyer and seller for some time. The sold business still has objectives, business plans, and projects that still need to be advanced. If there are exceptions, these can and should be called out during the pre-integration phase of the acquisition. Otherwise, it's full steam ahead!

The problem with this approach is that employees will likely feel a sense of uncertainty and loss of belief in a leader who takes this approach without having some strategic backing from the acquirer. Employees instinctively know that it is *not* business as usual. Acting as if it is so, only foments distrust.

If you are a leader in this situation and you know that your world is business as usual for your team, then by all means, say that. If, on the other hand, you hope it is but don't know, then it's best to share the value creation thesis and align your team to that expectation. Since the value thesis is mostly likely about realizing value, the leader's ability to align the work of the team toward value should serve to show the team how to do the same. The buyer wants the value of the business; anything the seller can do to help them obtain it should be welcomed as positive and supportive of their aim. Of course, the seller's leadership team still likely has direct obligations to the sold company at this time, but one of those objectives almost certainly will be to help close the transaction in a timely and successful manner.

The buyer wants the value of the business; anything the seller can do to help them obtain it should be welcomed as positive and supportive of their aim.

Stay focused on the goal. If you're in the seller's seat, live your best principles of leadership outwardly and transparently, modeling the way your team can create value post-acquisition.

Stop the presses

The alternate approach would be for the acquired team to just stop doing what they're doing in favor of waiting for permission out of fear of some future judgment. This wait-and-see attitude slows every aspect of the current business operations to nearly a halt. The mood of the company quickly becomes one where even the most ardently dedicated and engaged employees sense that their livelihoods are in peril.

Taking this approach creates more risk for all employees as the likelihood of the current business performing to plan diminishes each day while the wait-and-see stance slows decisions, projects, and new customer wins. Once this slowness settles into place, it is very hard to reverse as the most ambitious or mobile people will begin readying for a job search, and the rank and file will measure what their immediate leader actually does versus what they say. If you say, "We all need to row the boat" while you are swimming to a different shore, your actions will be recognized even if you don't intend them to be so.

This approach is a lose/lose for both buyer and seller. For the buyer, the transaction may not look as attractive as the progress and execution of the purchased business slows, potentially challenging the original business case that promoted the acquisition in the first place. When the deal does ultimately close and the reigns are handed from one leadership team to the next, the employee body will likely be highly unmotivated and much less engaged. This is very much like the athlete who sits out a season: returning to a previous level of performance is difficult even when highly motivated to do so.

For the selling company, the simple act of stopping the work in progress devalues it and can demoralize the teams performing it. As we wrote in *Respect the Weeds*, "Work is valuable when it is valued." We all invest tremendous intellectual effort and time to do the work we do. If it appears that the net result of our work will be simply to stop or wait for some uncertain future, it's going to be very difficult to be or feel motivated to continue doing it.

Seek approval

We don't pretend to speak for every leader here, but for ourselves. The art of gathering the facts, empathizing with an interested community, evaluating options, forming a plan, and executing on it… that's the reason why we enjoy what we do. We enjoy having the responsibility and authority to act. If either part is removed, be it presumed or imposed, the leader becomes either a "strategist" or a "doer." Neither role is necessarily bad, but post-merger leadership needs both to take decisive action to move a company forward with purpose.

This is not to say that anyone advocates the leader taking unwise or unilateral action without consulting with their constituents. However, a leader needs a sense of authority to do what is right within their area of control. If not, then why do we need them at all? Ask yourself, do decisions get made more rapidly when it's not clear who the decision maker actually is? The answer is simply no.

Another key challenge with having to seek approval for every decision, beyond being extremely slow and wasteful of time, is that it may be very unclear for a long time who in the acquiring company can actually approve a given set of decisions. This happens naturally as the buyer may not have fully thought through all the consequences and organizational structures post-close for some time. So, even if you feel like you must seek approval, there may be no person identified who can approve.

Our advice in this situation is simple: If the buyer demands that approval be given for most decisions of consequence, then the buyer needs to reconsider the leadership structure of the combined business unit, making it clear who and how decisions are to be made throughout the timeline from deal announcement to closing. The decision-making process may be very different over time as the buyer takes control of the acquired business. Initially, although not ideal, a set of rules on materiality needs to be established to avoid the lack of clarity on required approval. Over time, a committee of leaders from both companies may be formed to review and decide material matters. Ultimately, the acquiring company will be best served to simply implement its desired organizational structure and thus make clear the new lines of decision authority.

Take control (or attempt to)

Another post-merger survival approach is to take authoritarian control of the situation... or at least attempt to. Why say "attempt"? Simply put, companies are not democracies where one can run for office and gain control. They are more like occasionally benevolent dictatorships when it comes to organizational structure and authority. This said, it is normal for highly motivated leaders to aim to gain control of their future roles within an acquiring company.

Given that the reasons why a specific leader is chosen for their role within a leadership team are many and nuanced, including cultural fit, chemistry with the CEO or board of directors, compensation and incentives, taking an assertive role and taking control does not guarantee successful placement within the acquiring company structure.

The best approach is to align your actions and those of your team to the *value thesis* and then take charge in that direction. If the acquiring company is seriously considering the leader who takes this approach, they should be able to see that the actions taken are consistent with their desired outcomes.

As a cautionary note, this approach does not guarantee that the leader will ultimately join the new leadership team, as they may hope. It does, however, create the best opportunity for the acquiring company to see the leader in action and for the work of that leader's team to be best understood as contributing positively to the goals of the buyer.

Tune the Tensions, Don't Finesse Them

Companies are like living organisms in that they have a lifecycle. They are formed, they grow, they acquire new skills, they decline, adapt, return to growth, and struggle forward. Some companies pass the test of time and become seemingly immutable and unassailable while other companies succumb to the forces of their markets or fail to adapt to the ever-changing disruptive transformation brought on by technology, business models, and highly motivated entrepreneurs and new entrants.

In our experience, tension exists in all phases of this lifecycle and, if intentionally managed and optimized, can make all the difference between failure and success. Our careers have been dominated by companies that are for-profit in nature and hungry for growth. More importantly than growth, the companies we have worked for aspire to achieve *profitable* growth.

There may be a business model out there focused on a steady state, with no growth in revenues or profitability, but we have never worked for a company with that lack of ambition. No, for us, it has been all about competition and profitable growth. One way to achieve growth is through acquisition. There are many reasons for acquisition, ranging from adding products, supply chain or operational synergy, the introduction of disruptive innovation, or simply market consolidation. Regardless, acquisition is a component of almost all growth strategies. And being acquired brings all manner of tensions into stark relief and focus. Acquisitions are just a part of the fabric of business practices today. If you have not worked for a company that has made an acquisition or been acquired, it is very likely that you will do so someday soon.

We once acquired a small competitor, and immediately, the leaders of the acquired company were nervous, believing that we would shut them down due to "synergies" and simply take their customers. This was not part of the acquisition business case; we had been excited about the skills of several of their key leaders and their engineering team. Try as we might, we could not overcome this preconceived bias until we integrated their head of engineering into our technology leadership team. The individual had all the right skills, and, by adding him to our team as a leader, we showed the company that our words were sincere and supported by action. There were many other matters to address in the integration, but taking this action ensured employees that they would have an advocate who actually knew them and valued them for more than just the product they had built or the customers they had won.

We are not advocating the avoidance of difficult decisions when forming a combined team. Some people fit, and others just do not, but we are advocating that you keep an open mind and consider the overall benefits to the interpersonal tensions of the combined team should one of their own be elevated to the ranks of leadership.

If you've ever taken a university exam, you may recall that feeling when the proctor called out, "Pencils down," signaling that you had run out of time and all your diligent problem-solving had come to an abrupt end. To extend the analogy a bit, every company is taking a test of its operations every day. The goal is to perform to or exceed their plan. For the acquired company, the post-acquisition period can feel a lot like "pencils down." This is absolutely what the management of both companies needs to avoid. When you put your pencil down, you have done the work, and there's nothing left that you can do. You just have to wait for the result, which is no longer within your control. It's a miserable feeling regardless of how prepared you are for the test.

The aim of an acquisition has to be, in some way, about growth and value creation. Companies are made of people, and people have many competing objectives, all pulling on them all the time. For both parties in a transaction, great care must be taken to ensure that the pencils are moving all the time. It is imperative that questions are being openly asked and answered and that the goal to drive the individual and, ultimately, combined businesses is front and center as the priority of the employees of both parties. Incentives can help and must be aligned, but more importantly, the value creation thesis must be clear, the mission and vision must resonate in both camps, and the leaders need to have enough clarity about their futures to align their teams so the work continues.

In other words, this is not a time for "pencils down"! Instead, we must continue to address and *tune* the tensions, not just finesse them.

5

PRINCIPLES OF INTENTIONAL TENSION

We write this chapter imagining we could sit and talk with you, our readers, about the "and then what do I do" with the advice of this book. Growth is the ambition of every company, and sure enough, if you achieve greatness this year and you get your business growing, next year will welcome you with even greater expectations. Grow or die, right?

Faced with the constant balancing act of managing the cacophony of clamoring voices, daily emergencies, and escalations pulling our attention away from the higher ambitions of growth and leadership, how do you accomplish this year over year? The answer is that you cannot do it alone. It will take your entire company to work in unison, and it will take a real understanding of the systems of tension in your business. It will also take all the people in the company to join together in a common purpose and action.

Although we may not change our fundamental character, we may well embark on a journey of continued understanding, learning, self-improvement, and, most importantly, adaptation. As we wrote about in *Respect the Weeds*, we admire weeds for their fundamental ability to thrive in the most inhospitable environments through constant adaptation.

Be a Weed

You want to grow? Be a weed! Weeds all share four attributes that enable them to thrive and grow while being systematically hunted, pulled, poisoned, burned, and generally mistreated. Does that remind you of the competitive business environment within which your business must operate? How can you tap into your inner "weed" and continue to thrive?

Weeds all have deep perennial roots. If you have ever pulled a dandelion from the ground after a rain and you get the entire plant out of the ground, you can't help but see that the root is many times longer and more robust than the surrounding flower and leaves. This is a great example of the type of structure we are aiming for when designing and operating our business. We must be very well connected to the true sources of value that provide resources to the business. For the weed, it's water and the fact that the core of the plant lives in the roots. That's why we can dig and cut the plant, and it just grows back, sometimes even stronger, seemingly just to spite us.

What are the roots of value for your company? If you can answer quickly, that's a good sign. If not, then perhaps some real examination is due. Many have written about knowing the core metric for your business and focusing all attention on that. This concept points us in the right direction, but we need to extend this view to include the root sources of value in your business and not only an operational and financial metric. If you think a while about this, you will almost inevitably come to the conclusion that your people provide the only real source of sustainable value. The people are the roots of the company.

The skill and dedication of the company's core resources are the most critical and must be preserved. It is clearly understood that companies go through cycles of growth and retrenchment. The weed dies off and regrows. This, too, is often a reality for a business, but take great care not to cut too deep as doing so will ultimately kill the source of value over the long term. Obviously, if the company does not produce a financial return, then it is unable to sustain the people. Financial objectives are imperative. Delivering returns above bank rates comes from innovation, creativity, risk-taking, and dedicated people working in unison to accomplish common goals. Invest in the roots of your company, and you will be amazed at how resilient it will become.

But great people need to be working in unison for them to generate such resiliency. You must provide a common purpose to align and unite them. Common purpose is not a financial return objective. It is about what you do and the outcomes you aim to create for those you serve. Even if that outcome is of more or less consequence to the greater social good of the world, there must be some good from it in order to sustain it and for your employees to get behind it. This is the core of a mission, but not the type that is often written once and hung on the wall as corporate decor. A mission connects the work of the company to those it serves in a meaningful, valuable, and sustainable way. Provide such clarity, and your weed is beginning to sprout forth, perhaps ornery and rude, but determined to survive.

The roots of a weed resprout and recover quickly. The same root may well return the plant to your yard or crack in the pavement year after year. This is due to the uncanny ability to resprout. Weeds keep coming back, cycle over cycle, always investing resources in the depth of their roots while growing foliage and seeds to perpetuate their longevity. In the business world, we see this as inspiration for a perpetual and maniacal focus on the core

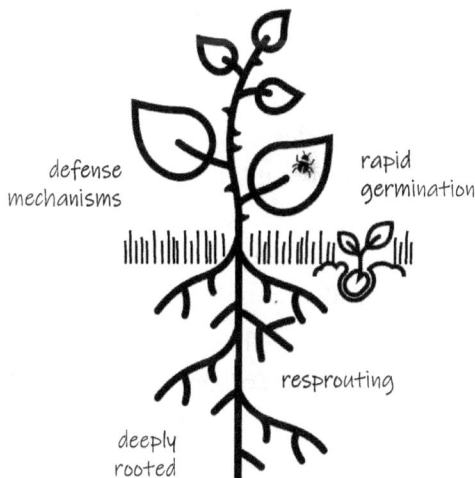

defense
mechanisms

rapid
germination

resprouting

deeply
rooted

value of the business while moving on from setbacks and losses quickly. You win some, and you lose some. The goal is to continue to play the game, sharing the wealth of returns to the roots and the plant to increase your odds of winning big over time.

Have you ever worked at a company that is sales-focused only? We have! That company rewards the win of the day only. If we win a big deal, we celebrate! If we lose a big enough deal, we cut expenses and then try to win the next big deal, now with an injured company. This type of organization puts all effort into the top-line growth of the business and leads to a culture of heroes and losers with no sustainable value beyond sales attainment.

We once worked in a company that had been led this way. We joined the business, having come from a different background, and found ourselves on the wrong side of key sales leaders when we promoted an approach of long-term innovation and sustained growth. In one instance, a sales leader, sitting in front of us and our executive team, started off on a personal rant about how we did not know where the company had come from, how things worked the way they worked there, how it was our job to give them what they wanted to drive sales over any other objective, and how not doing so immediately was a poor reflection on us as people! Our answer was, simply: "You don't know us well enough to lob such a presumptuous critique." This led to a meaningful conversation about tension in the business, objectives long term and short, and what the executive team would need to do to keep the positive aspects of the sales-driven culture while blunting the extreme single-focused tension it injected into the business overall. Over time, we won some, we lost some, but we did return the business to sustained growth and innovation while delivering on sales needs and expectations in a more balanced manner.

We will never be able to, or even want to, prevent tensions from forming within our company. The existence of tension forces us to adapt and grow. The absence of tension leads to a weaker company with little or no impetus to change for the better. We must also not ignore unproductive tensions or ones that run counter to our culture and long-term objectives. Doing so damages everyone involved in our venture and yields wasted energy and unneeded strife. External forces will always provide tension and a need to stay fit and competitive. If we are able to address those in unison and collaboration, aligned and fighting the external forces and competition together, our odds of success are greatly improved.

The existence of tension forces us to adapt and grow.
The absence of tension leads to a weaker company with
little or no impetus to change for the better.

Another highly annoying and admirable characteristic of weeds is that they have prolifically fast germinating seeds. Weeds spread their chances for successful propagation quickly in an almost unconstrained manner. This is by far more difficult a task in terms of a business as the seeds are the investments we make to increase the chances we may expand and grow our territory. This is a matter of point-of-view driven innovation as a process and the central theme of *Respect the Weeds*. Do not dismiss this critically important factor in sustainable business growth. Even if you fully manage all the unproductive tensions out of your business, time will change the value of your offer, commoditization will erode your price and share, and the seeds you would have planted for the future with the core resources of the company will be the reason you succeed over the long term. Failing to innovate creates tension with your markets, leading to the failure of a business over time.[9]

When upheaval occurs in business—an acquisition, market disruption, or loss of a key client—we need to "germinate" our new

---

[9] Tension mapping is a great tool to visualize the tension in your markets, with the relief of tensions between ecosystem players as a source of value creation.

value proposition quickly before our competitors steal all the sunlight.

Weeds also utilize specialized defense mechanisms. Weeds don't skimp on having thorns and prickly parts intended to discourage the ongoing assault against them. Weeds compete, inflict pain on those who attack them, and are resilient against so many obstacles that fell their more beautiful rivals.

Organizations that have found their tension sweet spot have also optimized their defense mechanisms. When a competitive threat arises, they are not prone to panic or finger-pointing. Instead, they are already tuned to respond quickly with their brand differentiators and unique selling points. They know instinctively that while they ponder a response or hire consultants, the market will have passed them by.

Prolific seeds, an ability to constantly adapt, the characteristic of resprouting roots, and a propensity to invest in its roots ultimately yield the plants that are most hated and that we also so greatly appreciate. The same admiration holds true for an enduring leader or a stubborn competitor. They use the fitness and fight of a weed to create a culture of survival and success in even the most hostile environments.

Treat Culture as a Verb!

Culture is so often talked about, yet really so misunderstood. Is it the summation of our actions and behaviors? Is it our aspiration? You will find the more people you ask, the more definitions you will get, and we assure you that there will be very little in the way of commonality that comes from the exercise. Given that we are by no means human resource experts, we aim to provide our definition in terms of the needed outcomes for growth.

In the way that a biologist views a Petri dish, we believe that culture should really be considered a verb or action word more than a noun in the context of organizational tension. Nouns are static; verbs are more about actions and outcomes. If you consider culture as the actions taken by the people of the business and those you have committed to take, then we have placed our culture in the hands of each individual to contribute and make it real. The roots of company culture come from how the values we profess encircle our behaviors; actions taken will either be within those bounded expectations or not. When we see actions taken that do not comport with our culture, we call them out and reinforce the expected actions instead. This means that culture is really what you do more than what you say.

Culture is really what you do more than what you say.

As leaders, we need to live the culture we aim to create. In doing so, our actions will serve as powerful examples for the actions we expect of our peers and teammates. We have all seen and felt when the stated culture is really only a façade, obscuring how things are really done, or when the true nature of the business does not track with and is not supported by the perfumed words of inauthentic leaders.

If culture is really the sum of the actions we take or don't take in accordance with our principles, then we may truly empower and expect the entire company to take an active part in its creation and fulfillment through its daily work. Like cells in the body, each is a part of the overall organism; each cell takes actions in accordance with its purpose and in the manner for which they are suited and tasked. Unlike cells, we all have minds and our own aspirations and needs. We profess that the cultural expectations, norms, and actions serve to align our thoughts and purpose in a manner consistent with our desired outcomes and mutual expectations.

In this way, too, the company may be alive with the buzz of the common culture of action and purpose. Yes, a living and vibrant organism. Each team member knows what is expected and acts in accordance with their self-interests in concert with those of the company. Think of all the presentations you may have endured discussing culture in nonactionable terms: Did they create alignment, or were they more like stuff we are expected to do because it's expected of us as individuals? Did you hear jokes about the cultural expectations quickly after they were shared? We've seen it all at this point in our careers. Actions are what you do, and culture-as-action ensures everyone is aligned and accountable—no room for bystanders in this approach.

We once worked for a great company in a cultural transition from noun to verb. Even the previously used nouns were not lived. The expected culture was summed up in very soft terms: "We aim to be a market leader in...." As a new leadership team, we took our shot at defining the verbs we wanted to see and would agree to live. For example, our first expectation of action started with "Be real." Being real meant being authentic. We expected and only accepted authenticity. No hidden agendas. No meeting-after-the-meetings to talk about what should have been shared in the first place. In short, *be real in the moment.* To be real is a committed state of action and sets the expectation of performance to an agreed set of cultural norms and desires.

Finally, the actions of leaders, whether they have the title or not, are often followed as exemplary. If it's acceptable to be rude in meetings, the company will become ruder. If it's acceptable to be unaccountable, the company will likewise slip into a lack of accountability. Be conscious of exemplifying the behaviors you want to see and be ruthless in not tolerating those that do not.

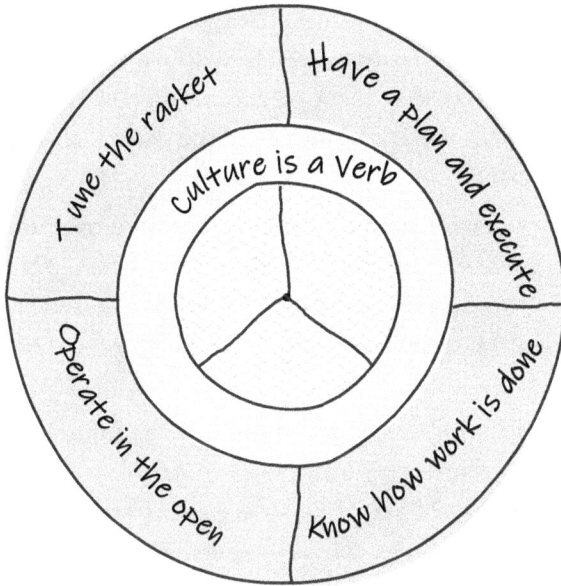

Know How You Create Value
(Not Think You Know)

It's time to look at your company, your function, and your department with fresh eyes, asking one key question (take a deep breath):

How do all of the organizations work together to achieve sustainable growth by delivering real and tangible value to your customers, so much so that they are not just willing but excited to choose your company and offer in the first place and pay you more year over year?

This task begins with understanding why your customers buy from and rely upon you and concludes—then and only then—with your internal alignment with those purposes.

Once we have a thorough understanding of *what* we offer and *why* it is of value, we next turn our attention to the *how* we do the work of the company. What are the primary processes of the company within and across each key organization? How do we communicate with our customers? How do we sell to them? How do we build products that meet or exceed market demands? It is important to do this work to understand the *how* for all of these key company functions.

Often, a company's internal processes evolve over time based on lessons learned. Every time a new problem occurs, it is resolved. How are the processes implemented to avoid or lessen the impact of that problem (and tensions) were it were to reoccur in the future?

The challenge with this approach is that the internal processes are simply a set of historical responses to problems encountered, more than a thoughtful set of well-designed frameworks of business processes tuned to deliver results and attain value. As acquisitions take place, for instance, more process and tension complexity is introduced. Over time, the result is less and less efficiency, which therefore requires more resources or human effort to accomplish the same outcomes.

We once took on a customer project to understand and improve the manner in which a telecommunications company planned and deployed its vast network of technologies. The value proposition was very clear: If we could conceive a process and set of systems to maximize the reuse of equipment rather than making new capital purchases, we would be compensated via the savings achieved. Further, if we could deliver a process to consolidate and eliminate unnecessary complexity and expense, we would be compensated for that, too. You can imagine how seriously we undertook this challenge. The project had a direct impact on the ability of our company to pay our teams and grow our business.

We started at the beginning by interviewing all the customer organizations that had anything to do with the process of building networks. We met with procurement, network planning, the deployment team leader, the operations teams, and many people who lived in trucks all day long doing the real work. The act of having these meetings and asking the simple question, "What happens when?" for any of the steps in their work was fascinating. No one really knew how the overall process worked, but every organization's leaders had conviction in the efficiency and effectiveness of their work—plus a whole lot of misgivings about the other teams around them. That might be human nature, but it was really amplified in this big-infrastructure environment.

We found that one customer team would do their part and pass it on to the next via many communication methods, including email, tickets, or paper printouts. The next team did not have all the information the prior team had, so they assumed the work was correct, even if it didn't really fit their expectations. The belief was, "We know we are getting a request; it's not based on complete data, but we will fill in the missing parts." This happened many times throughout the process, creating more and more drift from the true nature of the need. As a result, no one truly *owned* the current design, except perhaps those who maintained it physically. Over time, this led to a "just add and never remove" approach.

We expected the inefficiencies would have caused frustration and negative tensions, but we observed the opposite... *Total apathy.* Needless to say, we were able to refine this process through reengineering. The effects were truly transformative. As we were outsiders with a lot of questions, we could see their company process in a very broad sense. When our work was done, we left them with a map of their processes and organizations and a set of refinements in their approach that saved them millions of dollars each year.

Once we fully understand how the work of the company is done, we can assess and map the processes and tensions with an eye to alleviating those that waste energy and effort and tune the racket to be more sustainable and productive.

Clearly, our customer sensed there was a problem, but their analyses only looked one way, from each organization outward. The problem was always someone else's.

Look in the Mirror

We all see ourselves in the mirror as we ready for work and on video calls during the day, but we do so through a lens of bias. As we live our lives, not only do we change, but many of our perspectives do as well, as we learn and grow. Surely, the person we saw in the mirror in our youth is very different than who we see today. Rarely do leaders fully appreciate how they are perceived by others and those they lead, as those perceptions change over time with actions taken and their subsequent results.

As leaders, our actions are parsed and processed with much greater scrutiny than most. As we create a vision for our company and grow to realize that vision, we must balance the need for short-term expediency with that of long-term process excellence, organizational learning, and sustainable growth. If we are having a bad day, our team will notice and begin to conjure assumptions. Even the lack of a smile can be construed as an unintended warning to those surrounding us.

Leaders who can project kindness, fairness, and authenticity, even when a business is struggling, can create tremendous positive tension in our organizations and teams. That really is a big part of the job. Empathy starts with the awareness of the need for it and the realization that our employees have lives larger than just their work. Obviously, employment is a key part of each employee's life, but it's important to take into consideration that the sacrifices we ask or demand of our team come at a cost to them and their families. Given that we must ask employees to be dedicated to a certain degree of sacrifice, should we not do so with care and courtesy where possible?

The actions of a leader establish patterns for acceptable company behavior as well. If we start the day demanding—and not listening—we can expect that many will pick up our hints and may model such behaviors, perhaps unconsciously, if they believe that adversarial behavior is what is required to advance their careers.

We all are less articulate than we want to be at times. It is not practical to editorialize every word you speak, but if you realize that you will be perceived differently than you intended, take care to be your most authentic and empathetic self. Your company will follow over time.

Regularly taking stock of our skills is a critical responsibility of a leader. There are many ways to do this. Chief among them is to activate your sense of curiosity in all aspects of your business. Your best teachers are likely your employees and peers. Sometimes, we can improve our skills awareness by working with team members directly on a project. Admitting that you need to go to "school" is completely acceptable and expected in our view.

We once joined a company that had been in operation for a long time and had a lot of complexity in its technology and operations. Given its long history, it was very challenging to get our arms around what and how things were built over all those years, but we needed to do so in a rapid manner. The reality is that a new leader really only gets 100 days (or less!) to get up to speed and begin adding value. There are great books written on this topic also, but suffice it to say, the first 100 days set the tone for your time with an employer.

In this case, we took the "go to school" approach. The technology and operations teams wished to not only exhibit expertise in the technologies and evolution of the company but also know and understand the critical functions within the company. As a demonstration of transparency, we started attending the informal "university" of the company, with the functional teams as our professors. The outcome was fantastic! We quickly became trusted members of the team and not just "management." Each presentation further solidified our working knowledge and allowed us to catch up quickly.

The thirst for skills enhancement and knowledge needs to extend beyond the current borders of your functional area. So, take time to learn the other parts of the business as you continue to perform your job-specific function. Doing so makes the company stronger and the tensions more resolvable as one party can more accurately understand the challenges of the other and the implications of their work.

Enterprise awareness is particularly important as disruption is now part of the normal flow of business. You are currently being disrupted all the time, whether you realize it or not. Be prepared, learn all you can, and keep looking for new opportunities to enhance your skills inside and outside your organization and company walls.

Progress Over Perfection

It was Einstein who said, "The definition of insanity is doing the same thing over and over and expecting different results." True then and true now. However, organizational learning can be very slow, and the same problems seem to pop up repetitively. Tensions build, the big meeting or a blow-up takes place, and the issue is resolved that day only to take place again down the road.

This is due to several factors that must be carefully managed to drive improvement in long-term performance rather than just acceptance of the status quo. Using our analogy of the tennis racket, we need to actively tune and refine it over time. Even the best racket will lose tension, or perhaps the player will need to improve their performance based on the conditions of their next match.

In business, this really comes down to embracing and embodying an approach of continuous improvement.[10] Teams are organized into functions, and those functions tend toward process development and refinement over time. This is a good and expected aspect of organizational planning and behavior.

We must redouble our efforts and emphasis on process development and refinement not only within the individual teams but, more importantly, between them. *As if* this were not already hard enough, we must also be willing to change the processes over time

---

[10] See *Respect the Weeds*, Chapter 4: Applying Principles to Drive Meaningful Change

as our environment and circumstances change. In many ways, the learning of a team is stored in its process and records. No one works forever. As custodians and employees, we must plant the seeds for evergreen renewal and improvement.

It is very tempting, in the heat of the battle, to just fix the problem at hand. We all do it, right? And sometimes, we need to do this in response to the many and varied challenges the business faces each day. We also know that this is not how we drive continuous improvement. Having the discipline after the fires are put out to look back, understand the root causes of what took place, and establish a process, training, or personnel adjustment is the only way we can keep looking forward and not over our shoulders all the time. The hardest part, then, becomes changing what we have created. Inventors fall in love with their inventions because they represent the cunning and novelty of their thoughts and ideas. We, too, can become stuck in the ways of working that we have created.

Business processes must align with desired business outcomes, ones that are stated in a manner that their achievement demonstrates greater chances for sustained growth and long-term success. What you measure gets done. We have all heard and seen this in action. What this means for us here is that we really need to create processes and measures that drive the fulfillment of valuable outcomes for the overall business first. If one team is fantastic at delivering its part of the value chain, but the others are incapable of picking up the work and selling, delivering, and supporting it, we won't grow or, potentially, even survive.

Here's an example to illustrate this point. We once worked for a company that had thousands of customers on hundreds of platforms, each customized and configured a bit differently from one another. Having thousands of customers is a great problem to have, but the wide variance in implementation and customization presented a massive set of challenges. Roadmaps, enhancement requests, upgrades, training, support, and many other matters were all extremely challenging and less profitable than desired. Very few customers had the same requests, and our ability to invest in a common product became more and more difficult as we grew.

The vast majority of customers were satisfied, but there was a measurable percentage that were not. We measured quality and help desk tickets and a myriad of other metrics, but none really told the story. We needed to understand and address customer satisfaction across a diverse set of customers with a lot of variances in how our systems were utilized.

After a number of iterations and evaluations of our process, we learned a key but simple fact: What we viewed as a priority was not viewed the same way by each of our customers. Being a very engineering-oriented company, we prized (and radically prioritized) availability and uptime. Meanwhile, our customers expected that, but they also expected their enhancements done in short order. It was really a matter of perspective. Once we were able to look critically at our own process for gathering customer requirements, funding, and priority, we were able to direct resources in a more balanced manner to meet both the availability and timeliness objectives and improve the overall satisfaction of our customers and ourselves.

Getting to these process refinements came from a lot of tension and misunderstanding between internal teams, but in the end, having used the voice of the customer as a clarifying truth, we were able to achieve a far better result than any organization alone could have done. In this case, the desired business outcome was to increase the number of delighted and well served customers while growing our revenue.

Key to this example and practice of continuous improvement is that it needs to be top-down *and* bottom-up. Meaning, the strategy of the company needs to exert and establish a tension for excellent results measured in business execution, while each organization needs to establish and refine their process in support, paying close attention not only to localized optimization but also to the macro (enterprise-level) systems of tension within which they operate.

You can go too far, and often, due to frustration, we do so. For example, when two teams are meant to work together but the boundaries and trust relationships are not clear, it is common to create RACI charts for each team so they may achieve clarity and reach an agreement on the key responsibilities of each party. The RACI model is a useful tool that defines who is Responsible, Accountable, Consulted, or Informed for a given set of objectives. This can be a useful tool to gain alignment and clarity. Where it can go too far is when so many columns and rows of work items are defined down to low-level tasks that the model becomes impossible to manage and is really more like a contract than a working agreement. The purpose of agreements is to gain alignment, while contracts are typically used to hold people accountable. There is a big difference in intention and practice between the two approaches. So, create a RACI if useful, but only do so to create alignment and agreement between teams for the purpose of relieving negative tensions and creating effective ones. If the work is moving back and forth frequently, look again at the organizational structure and the process itself for simplification. There are no hard rules here, but simpler is generally more efficient and effective.

Remember, organizations are collections of like-tasked individuals. Each person may well have their own objectives and complaints, but those personal conflicts and biases should not find their way into convoluted RACI agreements. As leaders, we are expected to look above the petty and personal and focus on the growth of the business while leading our teams to resolve tensions every day in the normal course of business.

Transparency and Accountability

If you have read our previous book, this part will come as no surprise. You need to have a plan. You need to work out what's important and what your primary objectives are. You need to take the time to identify your specific goals and who will be accountable for executing them. And, of course, you must clearly establish how you will measure your goals to ensure success.

Once you've taken these steps—which, to be effective, must be done in collaboration and consultation with your team—identify the accountable leaders who will put your collective plan into action and execute it every day to deliver the desired results of your business strategy.

We previously worked for a company that was in the midst of turmoil resulting from a difficult financial transformation and a set of disruptive marketplace actors who had commoditized the value propositions that had built the enterprise. When we arrived at this company, we saw disorganization and a lack of clarity as to how success would be achieved and how the company would return to sustained growth.

Taking our own advice, we established a functional team and modeled our plan after the aforementioned VSEM model: vision, strategy, execution priorities, and measurable metrics. Each team leader was assigned a core area of responsibility and a set of objectives they needed to support in order for the overall organization to achieve its objectives. In other words, the plan was designed so that success was measured both by each individual team and as a collection of teams that would create the ultimate result of market growth.

Along the way, we learned that the company really needed to understand the *benefits* of the metrics instead of just the metrics themselves, so we modified our plan to be VSE<u>B</u> (for benefits). No plan is worth the effort to create it unless understood by all and executed. Awareness was achieved by printing our plan on large format printers and hanging it on the walls throughout our office area. We also published it on the company's internal intranet and provided monthly updates on our progress to the whole company. Updates included the setbacks and challenges we had experienced and the pivots we had made. Just doing these things created an expectation of accountability within the organization and a unified focus on delivering for the business.

Eventually, our peer organizations began creating their own plans in concert with ours and asking even more refined questions about how the overall systems of tensions of the business fit together to create sustained growth. This is a great example of transparency and accountability in action. Stating your plan and being accountable to it is essential to achieving anything in an intentional manner. We aim for intentional transformation based on the tensions we exert on ourselves and the overall enterprise. Anyone can get lucky, but real transformation comes from intention, and intention is worthless without planned action and execution.

Publicizing our plan created a degree of awareness that had never existed before in this business. We ran the technology organization, which had primarily been viewed as a cost of doing business, expensive, and very difficult to manage. By stating our plan, we were able to speak in terms of the objectives of the business so that the activities we undertook could truly be seen in the context of sustainable growth. And so, we went from being problematic to being strategic.

One thing is for certain: If you take the time to establish a plan, identify the leaders who will be accountable for the execution of each aspect of the plan, and you are transparent in your progress reporting on the execution of the plan, you will have created a degree of accountability unmatched by most enterprises today. Accountability drives ownership and execution. Execution and the outcomes it creates are the currency of an organization.

Accountability drives ownership and execution. Execution and the outcomes it creates are the currency of an organization.

Simply put, if your organization says what it's going to do and does it and can prove it time and time again, you will be trusted because you are *trustworthy*... You are worthy of someone's trust. If you can propagate clear planning and accountability throughout your organization as you focus on continual process improvement, your chances of success will be much greater to achieve growth.

Furthermore, by stating your plan, you open yourself up to the opportunity for constructive criticism and improvement. Note that we said *constructive* criticism. Criticism for the sake of it or for political games within organizations that are attempting to grow cannot be tolerated in any way. By taking the approach outlined here, any politics will fall away as the visibility and transparency of your plan and its execution will cut through the noise and show the true value of the work you have undertaken. When you experience resistance to change, which you most certainly will, take the high ground and rely upon the benefits you've achieved for the business to be the example for why your approach should prevail.

It's Up to You

It's up to you...This simple statement is intended to be a sobering one. No matter where you sit within an organization or a company, the success or failure of the company, in part, is up to you. Success depends on your actions and the decisions you make or don't make each day. We should all consider our employment within a business as a true privilege and an act of trust on the part of the business owners, be they private investors or public shareholders. They have placed their trust in you to make decisions that are in their and your mutual best interest to create a vibrant enterprise and sustained growth.

If we view our employment as a privilege and our access to it as an act of trust by our shareholders, then we must take responsibility for leading our business each day in a manner consistent with this privilege and trust.

We must invest our attention on eliminating dysfunction wherever we see it, whether that be in our own leadership style and teams or in the business processes and systems of tensions that make up the complex matrix of organizations so organized to do the work of the business.

We must set examples ourselves for what excellence and execution look like. We must be accountable to ourselves and our peers, and we must bring our best selves to the activities of the business each day so that our energies may be put to the purpose of creating growth and a sustainable enterprise.

When we have bad days, we must look at them as examples of how to improve, and when we have great days and experience great wins with our teams, we must celebrate these victories while also learning from them. This is the nature of seeing a business as a *living organism* created by each of us striving for the common purposes for which we're employed. Simply put, we must set the example for how we want to see our peers lead their daily activities. And we must look in the mirror and constantly ask ourselves, "Are we doing all that we can to elevate our skills and those of our teams?"

We must not allow ourselves to become the autocrats who demand conformance and execution and assume that our employees will simply fall in line and do as we say. We must be humble enough to recognize that we don't know the best way to achieve all the goals of all the company objectives ourselves. That it's going to take a team of highly motivated and incentivized people working in collaboration to create and relieve tensions that make us stronger and enable us to deliver for our customers.

The transformative leader is humble and authentic and real. It doesn't matter whether you're a project manager or at an advanced stage of leadership in your career. You can be humble and authentic, and you can be an example for all those who are around you. We assert that transformation comes from within because the organizations themselves already know, in many cases, how to best deliver unprecedented outcomes for their constituents. As leaders, we must listen and be humble and take advice when it fits and challenge it when we see it does not. We must undertake a process of constant learning and self-improvement and encourage the same from our team members each day. We must "go to school." And we must be interested enough to learn not only our functional area but also those of the overall business so we may understand and be a truly vibrant and contributory member of it.

Take the time to create an actionable strategy to achieve measurable objectives through a transparent plan in which everyone can see they have a part in achieving. We have been building the elements of your strategy throughout this book, illustrated in full now as the Intentional Tension Model (Figure 23).

Figure 23. Intentional Tension Model

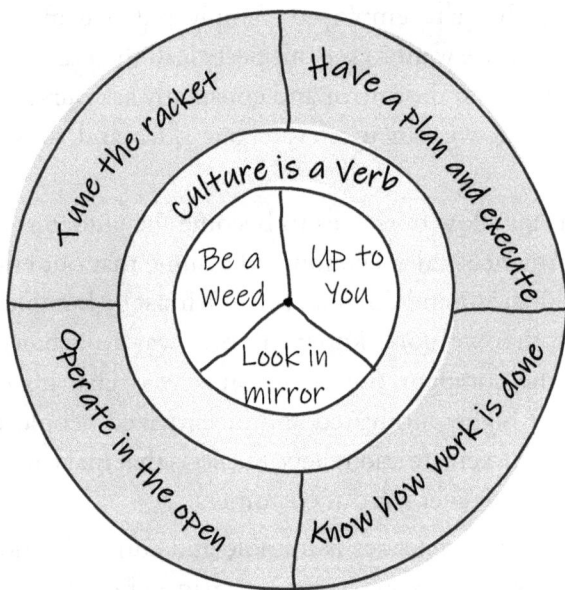

Make it as clear as you can, but do not steer away from complexity. The world is a complex and changing place, and our ability to continue to learn is paramount to our ability to survive in a changing environment. It is often said we must "dumb it down" or express the complexity in terms of spreadsheets only... This is a mistake. The goal is to find the simplest form of a strategy that still expresses its true form, which is likely far more complex and nuanced than a spreadsheet will ever be able to describe.

Our best advice is to sketch out an illustration that captures all those spreadsheets, requirements lists, and PowerPoints. A picture truly does convey a thousand words.

If you take the opportunity to consider and implement even a few of the ideas and concepts within this chapter, you will be a changed leader, and you will be perceived as one who is open to change and steadfast in your commitment to achieving the common goals of the company no matter where you sit within it.

6

TRANSFORMING TENSIONS

Tension, good and bad, can often be mapped directly to business plans, good and bad. Poor planning leads to organizational chaos or, perhaps worse, organizational apathy. Even when all of your strategic intent, investment intent, and cultural intent are well aligned, how often are they conveyed to people through a static, uninspiring business plan? In this chapter, we hope to show the connection between the business plan and organizational tension—the *intentional* tension that needs to be conveyed by a plan and how a plan can be a tool to transform the tensions in your organization.

Organizational tensions: ignore them at your peril!

Growth targets are set—or better yet, *determined*—with thoughtful research at hand. Investors are counting on growth; that's the only reason they would invest in a for-profit company. They are counting on us all to deliver this year, quarter after quarter, but what they really need and want is sustainable growth over time. Very few companies can deliver breakout success in their first year, and sustain that over ten years, without an exceptionally focused plan, a ton of execution, and a learning organization full of motivated people.

Any manager can drive a single-faceted outcome in the short term. If you have any degree of control and responsibility and budget authority, you can get an outcome. We need to hit our EBITDA this year, and sales are fixed or declining?!? Reduce the number of employees? We can create a "cost optimization" project and swing the axe. The net effect may well be short-term cost reduction, but the missed deliverables and innovations required for next year's growth may well no longer be deliverable.

In business, leaders frequently say, "It's easy to cut costs. We'll just eliminate employees." It actually is not easy, and it should not become so, as we are likely doing harm to each affected person's life and livelihood… harm that is visible to those who remain in the company. The implementation of this approach is fraught with organizational pain, politics, and potential legal challenges.

Approximating the future based on what is known about the past and anticipating the potential disruptions or changes to the pattern repeating is a very difficult thing to do. How do we create the plan of record for the growth of a business in transition, one facing the uncertainty of new competitors and technology transformation, emerging opportunities, the commoditization of core business over time?

The answer is in front of us all every day and comes down to moving from the known to the unknown, in an algorithmic way—tapping into a programmatic process in a consistent manner.

We first must identify the business(es) we are in. This may sound easy enough, but you will find that the business you think you are in may actually be very different from the one(s) you truly are in. For example, we once worked for a company that was in the stated business of creating custom-finished physical goods. Great! "We help companies make things and distribute them to the parties that buy them." Sounds easy enough. All the attention of the IT team was focused on the procurement, inventory, supply chain, logistics, and distribution of these goods.

Taking a deeper look, though, revealed that the company actually was much more than that. The company designed the goods and thus had the need for a creative department. They needed to make some of these goods with companion software, so it was also a custom software development business. Not identifying the business you are really in makes it hard to identify and monetize all the hidden potential for value creation and growth.

For each of the lines of business you have now understood and decided to remain in, you will struggle with a formula, an algorithm for growth. The financial modeling part is tedious but can be done based on current business performance and the backlog you have already committed to customers. Then comes the hard part....

You have to have an informed point of view about the needs of the customers your line of business serves. You need some insight and some vision and a strong dose of innovation to grow from where you are now to a future that you hope will thrill your investors and constituents.

Our book, *Respect the Weeds* [Chapter 5: Change is Hard], provides a strong process for a point-of-view-driven creation and innovation process. Establishing a lasting, evergreen business requires a rational, continuous innovation process as a fundamental element of your growth planning. Plan on innovation based on the understanding of needs informed by real research and empathy with your buyers and customers. Understand your competitors and how they and you make money. Understand how you create value and where the lines of business really make money.

Once you have this in hand, look to develop a strategic roadmap—a simple, fact-based plan of what customers will need over the coming years based on *the why*, which is informed by your points of view and research.

With these thoughts now clear, you iterate in the innovation process, creating and selecting the ideas that have the best chance to fulfill your growth objectives.

This sounds very straightforward, but it is extremely difficult to do as, realistically, we never have pure facts and pure financial models that will tell us exactly what to do and when. Instead, we have a series of risk-based investments to make to enable us to capitalize on our view of the opportunity to serve the current and future needs of our customers.

We also need to select the period over which we will project our view of future growth. Most often, the expectation is three to five years. One year can be budgeted for. Predicting the future beyond a few years is more like crystal ball gazing unless your business is extremely predictable. In our experience, there are not many highly predictable businesses that are undisruptable over an extended period of time. Therefore, you need to plan to pivot along the way. You need to invest in platforms and products that are built to be iterated on and evolved as customer demands change over time. In essence, you are building tension mitigation into your economic engine.

We posit in this book that you must create sustainable and intentional tension throughout your enterprise in order to create sustainable growth. A business with too much tension is a mess of politics and conflict, while one free of tension will lack the will and ways required to drive outcomes and progress.

Sustainable, profitable growth is the pinnacle challenge of business leadership. Tension mapping and an action-culture with a clear and verifiable innovation plan are your best approach to summit this mountain.

So, how do we sustain a culture of innovation, productive tension, and action? That's a very tall order for any leader. The answer is really very simple. Lead with intention, humility, and facts; set the expectation for these outcomes; and pay people for attaining them. You must live them yourself, of course, but in doing so, you (yes, you) set the example for what is expected every day.

When you have bad days, move on from them, and when the company does, learn from them and do not enter the blame storm. Learn and move forward. If there is malice and blame, deal with it privately.

How do companies learn? People may well actually learn from every challenge, and that is a great start. Make sure to reinforce that culture and hold those out-of-comfort-zone meetings where the topics are "What happened? What did we expect? What did we do or not do?" and "What did we learn?" Also, make sure to take the critical and most important step to ask the teams to review these things for the purpose of creating processes, procedures, and technologies to avoid the same circumstances in the future. Make the effort to force organizational learning and process improvement and be willing to reinvent what you have created if it no longer serves the company optimally.

Lastly, continuous learning doesn't stop when tensions are stressed by business cycles and unforced errors.

The Q4 Blame Shuffle

Pressure increases as the year progresses. This is just a reality in a for-profit business. The yearly investments must be repaid in the form of growth and profits. As the quarters tick by, deal closings, once forecasted for a given period, oftentimes slip for perfectly valid reasons and sometimes less valid reasons as well. Regardless, quarter four typically determines if the overall year will be measured as a success or failure.

In a purely product business, if the products are fit for purpose and available to sell and deliver, the bulk of the pressure falls to the sales and operations teams. However, technological products are sold on a roadmap and, in our experience, are often sold outside of specification. Worse yet, they are often delivered out of operational specifications as well. The result sets up a very potent set of tensions between the quarterly pressures to deliver financial returns per plan owned by the commercial and operational teams and that of the product and production teams.

While success has many parents, failure, as they say, has none. Never is this more evident than the moment a customer contract starts going off track and the sales teams take to blaming the product for all its problems and challenges. (This has happened to us so frequently that it's difficult to quantify fully, but it is a real opportunity to reflect on one's leadership.) The natural initial response is only human nature: settle in for the fight and just dredge up every hypocrisy and weakness of the contentions being levied by our friends in quarters one, two, and three.

This is human nature, but it's not the best of human nature. We must fight this reaction to win at all costs. It's important to remember to be empathetic even when those we are trying to understand may, in fact, be injuring the relationship they have with us. To us, this is the ultimate act of leadership. Instead, we should take the opportunity to become crystal clear on what was asked and delivered. Take further actions to assure our peers that while we agree with their assessments that have merit and will expend our energy on generating a positive result, we do not agree with or accept their unfair assessments. In doing so, we may teach, by example, how to relieve tension and eliminate politics.

In the end, we are all paid from the same purse. Contemplating retribution for the insults delivered and felt may be an instinctive and justifiable emotional response, but it will not help anyone, let alone our most important stakeholders, our customers.

This is a fine line, though.... Disagreeing with an unfair complaint is still an imperative to ensure that the record is accurate. Our goal is for each organization to take full responsibility for its accountability without hesitation or politics or wasted energy. Visualize it. Map it.

When you encounter this phenomenon, address it directly to the parties waging their campaign. Call them out, but then move on to what you and they may be able to do to deliver to each other and the customer. Refocus the joint team on what success looks like specifically and who can contribute to creating this outcome, then determine what process improvements may be implemented to avoid the circumstance going forward.

Again, this is hard to do. Sometimes, leaders will react in kind, take the rhetoric down, and collaborate; other times, they may dig deeper into their dysfunction and simply raise the level of conflict and tension. If the latter approach is taken, our advice is to be prepared and meet your peers on the battlefield until it is likewise clear in their view that the first option is the only logical one to pursue.

Trusting, high-functioning people and the teams they lead will act with consistency in times of plenty or scarcity. If Q4 is coming and the pressure is on, and you have a set of serious product and customer challenges, and you are worried you may not make it without some extraordinary effort on the part of the organizations that support you, own it. Reach out, share the problem humbly, and ask for support. We bet you will be pleased with the outcome this creates versus the Q4 blame shuffle.

It is very, very tempting to play the short-term game as we strive to create sustainable value. Ask yourself: How many times have you made the tradeoff between the quarter and the year in terms of financial results? How many times have you looked at that cash cow and counted on it to deliver next year? How many times have you measured the incubating seed of growth against the core business margin and decided not to invest or not invest at the required rate? All of these decisions are understandable in isolation but are in direct conflict with the core objective of sustainable growth.

We must be willing to stick our necks out, to stretch for the next higher goal, and set this expectation for the entire company as we tune the racket every day. These activities and norms need to become the instinctive actions of the enterprise and its leaders.

They will follow if you will lead. So, start now! Set up that meeting between the leaders of your team, ask them to read what is written here, and iterate. Log off the Teams meeting and go meet with your customers. Buy the research paper. Start an innovation team and fund them. The value of this work will be measured in the outcomes your actions create. (Above all, sustainable business growth comes down to the people... Treat them with this level of trust, respect, and accountability, and they will reward you tenfold.)

Companies form, grow, struggle, scale, and become great, or they do not. Even the best companies, over time, can easily lose their discipline and execution as inefficiency and lack of clarity creep in. Tensions rise, productivity falls, and they either reset and return to growth or fail. What separates the winners and losers is the essential truth that sustainable growth is only possible through sustainable and ongoing leadership and intentionally managing the tensions of the business through organizational learning and ongoing improvement.

The Tension of Self

There is an adage that says, "It's lonely at the top." That sounds a bit dramatic, but it is true in our experience. Leadership, for all its opportunities to express one's most authentic and actualized self, can be a very isolating and, yes, lonely occupation. Leaders are faced with the challenges of leading a team or organization through the perils and pressure of daily business and the burdens of managing a complex set of internal tensions. It is also rarely clear exactly what to do to *orchestrate* tensions.

Leaders are people, too, and the only difference between them and other employees is the degree to which investors have entrusted care and control to them. Having said that, it's human nature to look for problems in others rather than to first look at oneself as a source of tension creation or apathy… to look in the mirror, as we discussed earlier. But it is through that lens of self-reflection that we can also ask, as leaders, how the individual in our care sees their role in creating or abating tensions amongst and between their teams.

As the tensions of daily work increase, the levels of performance between individuals separate more clearly, especially when viewed from the perspective of an executive leader. Some people just perform and deliver better and more consistently than others. We continually strive to coach and improve overall performance through the art of leadership and mentoring, but the one thing that may never be rectified through coaching is desire or the drive to achieve. Some people step up to a new level of performance while others either cannot, or worse, choose not to do so.

In our experience, team performance never increases linearly. As a team establishes goals and starts to achieve them, confidence increases, experience is accumulated, and the real performance level is established. As more is achieved, more is expected because it becomes self-evident that more is possible. This is a virtuous cycle and can exponentially accelerate overall output. There are limiting factors, of course, such as time, attention, external considerations of other teams, and competition for resources. These all must be managed in concert with the desire to take your team to its optimal level of performance, rooted in their tension of self.

It is also true, though, that as some team members grow, others may not or may not grow at the same rate. The level of competence of a team may increase, and some of the members who were performing well before the transformation now struggle to perform at the higher level. Experience has shown that in the vast majority of cases, the only real limitation of a person's performance is their own desire and perhaps some encouragement and investment on the part of their leaders and peers.

Sometimes, however, people just give in to tensions... or just give up.

Quiet Quitting

Quiet quitting is a term that was introduced during the great migration away from offices and to our homes as places of work during and after the COVID-19 pandemic. Quiet quitting can be difficult to see as employees are now more remote than ever and may not even live close enough to an office to come onsite and commune with the organization in person. If an employee does not attend meetings, does not log their time, or starts to fail to deliver on commitments, these are all indicators that the employee may be quietly quitting... disengaging from the team and the work.

Obviously, this is completely unacceptable behavior and must be dealt with quickly should it emerge. The impact on the overall team is significant and negative as well. If the team sees that their peers are not delivering and that this is accepted by leadership, they, too, may well become disenfranchised and take the same approach.

What are the causes of quiet quitting, and why has this emerged as a real phenomenon now? We believe the root cause is a lack of engagement and effective leadership demonstrated by people leaders who simply do not possess the skills to lead remote teams. Sure, there are employees who behave badly at times and must be removed. But when this phenomenon runs deeper, it is more likely a reflection on leadership or the lack thereof.

One approach we have introduced to intentionally manage the tension of our teams and eliminate quiet quitting is to hold "sync time" meetings (as in synchronization). Yes, we are a bunch of geeks who love technology terms as applied to real-life situations. The agenda of a sync time meeting is literally just to connect as a team and address any open matters that don't fit neatly into project calls and team meetings. Sometimes, our sync time meetings are direct and focused on a problem; at other times, they are simply to recognize a job well done or something else that may be top of mind.

We don't use these meetings as social engagements. We ask that people do that on their own time. Rather, the action of creating a virtual water cooler alone has significantly improved communications and helped us avoid the quiet quitting phenomenon.

We also advocate an approach to leadership that is more conversational in nature over the "set it and forget it" goal-oriented management approach of times past. For sure, the day you set the yearly goals for a team, they will have changed in some way by the close of business. It is important to have clear goals, but it is more important to stay connected to those expected outcomes and those who will be tasked with delivering them.

Tension management is not about indiscriminately creating stress or competition. The act of relieving unproductive tension is just as valuable as that of creating productive tension. Take great care not to confuse these two approaches or risk value destruction.

We are *intentionally* designing and structuring tensions that will empower and bond teams to a common purpose and shared objective.

Setting organizational expectations with accompanying measurable outcomes is a very common practice in well-run businesses. Every team needs to know not only its purpose or mandate but also what it is expected to deliver, to whom, and by when. Without this degree of formality, larger organizations struggle to accomplish their mandate and often fall into complacency and wasteful behavior. Managing tension intentionally starts by looking at yourself within your organization and ensuring that the mandate, processes, and internal and external customers are clear, and then establishing and sharing a plan to meet and serve the objective with published metrics that describe and motivate attainment.

The ultimate test of your job of orchestrating tensions is how your organization carries on if you are no longer there to lead them.

When Leaders Leave

Change creates tension, and no more so than at a time of leadership change. We have been honored to lead rich careers working for numerous companies. Ultimately, we left each as the result of change. Either we made a change in career direction, or left following the close of a sale transaction, or accepted a better opportunity. Regardless of the reason, we left and shifted our attention and effort to a different company and purpose.

It is fascinating to us what happens to a team once a true servant leader has left. The hope, of course, is that nothing else changes except the person at the top, with their different personality and style, and that the change is a source of positive tension. This is rarely the case, though.

To use an analogy, metal that is exposed to force may well flex but not truly change shape in any permanent way. External tension applied by a leader to a team who either doesn't fully buy in or has not shared galvanizing experiences together really does not change the shape of an employee's views on the work or the manner in which it is done. For teams that view their leader as just a boss who sets expectations and measures results, when a new boss comes along, they snap to the will of the new pressure, and the job becomes just a job.

Teams that have gone through a lot together tend to remain tight and ride through a change in leadership without much disruption. These teams who have led together under times of great duress and challenge tend to have truly been changed not only from the tension of the leadership but also the pressure and heat of the challenging shared experiences. For us, challenging experiences like a cyber event, service outage, or even something more benign such as an office or data center move, are experiences that bond teams and bring them together in a way that forever changes them in a positive way. Teams that fight the good fight together? They are the ones accumulating skills, resolve, and resilience.

During such times, principled leaders prove not only themselves but the value of their principles as they lead in a consistent manner under tremendous pressure every day. The role of a great leader is to improve the skills of those they lead and, likewise, to leave the companies for which they work forever improved. They do this by optimizing the tensions *structurally*, not opportunistically.

Structural tension setting is not lived in an org chart but in the cells of the corporate organism:

Remember what we have done together here, and learn from both the good and difficult times. Treat each other well, as no one else will do so if you don't, and aim to always improve yourself and leave the company better when you move on. Lead with your head and heart and with your principles on full display, and you may walk away head up and proud.

Finding the right balance between the heart and mind can be one of life's constant struggles; so, too, can finding the right balance of operational tensions.

Amplify or Attenuate

In physics, we describe the characteristics of waves as they act upon one another. Simply put, waves of energy expressed in any form, the ocean, or the strum of a guitar, either amplify (join and increase in magnitude) or attenuate (work to diminish in magnitude) each other. Leaders either amplify or attenuate the energy of an organization and, as such, must be very careful to choose when to do so intentionally. How do you do this? Amplify the positive energy and attenuate the negative. This does not mean ignoring brutal truths and hard facts. The facts are the facts, and ignoring them will only lead to bad outcomes and negative consequences. Attenuating the negative organizational energy surrounding the facts gives the organization and leader more clear focus and energy on resolving the risk in a collaborative manner. Sounds simple and easy, but it is, in practice, very difficult to do every day, good and bad.

Have you ever found yourself in a meeting where everyone is talking over one another, blame is flying from one party to another, and nothing is getting accomplished? Then, the "leader" raises their voice and joins in but with more authority, assigning the blame. We have, unfortunately, been to many meetings like this. Once the leader takes this approach, collaboration to resolve or improve the matter is likely impossible. Each person in the room either agrees or not with what has been said and likely shares nothing more for fear of reprisal or worse. Time, energy, and collaboration are lost in this environment.

We once worked for a company that constantly sold and committed to delivering solutions to its customers that it had never designed before. This is often the case in technology companies. But the act of committing to something that has no proof of viability requires a degree of transparency far greater than most salespeople can stomach. Still, commitments are then made (by sales), requirements are not clear, the customer believes they have paid for a solution, and the engineering team is expected to just deliver. This has been the story of so many difficult and sometimes failed projects. Finance would never commit to a level of financial performance unsubstantiated by results, so why would any other organization act in this manner? The simple act of one party making a commitment for another with limited or no interaction is a case in point of unbalanced tensions in a company. In our view, successfully delivering on a strategy really comes down to incentives and trust. When one party has incentives that stretch another, transparency improves trust among the parties, while the lack of transparency builds resistance and unproductive tension, often resulting in wasting precious time.

Inevitably, projects like this take longer than hoped for, cost more, and often lead to very negative customer experiences. In the case described above, we needed the revenue; therefore, the company was hungry for almost any deal it could take to fill the void in the year's planned performance. Sure enough, the customers started to notice that they were working with a project manager instead of a technology leader. The requirements literally ballooned to almost tenfold the intended scope. Success was poorly defined and so never quite met.

In order to right the ship, the CTO and key heads of the technology organization took the project over directly and managed to get it delivered. The customer was engaged every day in a stand-up meeting for many months. The meeting always started the same: "We really should fire you guys" or some variation on that theme, but the message was clear: Delivery was met with setbacks and a multitude of unexpected and unwanted consequences. With some drop-everything, all-hands-on-deck efforts, we delivered an operational solution.

To make it worse, the project was touted as a success! While we pulled off a miracle, it came at an extreme cost to the company and employees and was close to failure at several points in its delivery. This is not the model for a well-balanced and optimally functioning organization. For the customer, even though they got the result in the end, this was neither their expected project delivery cadence nor an acceptable risk profile.

We need to face the brutal truth that businesses, like ourselves as individuals, are full of contradiction, and making isolated decisions for the sake of expediency and control is a shortcut to failure more often than success.

We need to face the brutal truth that businesses, like ourselves as individuals, are full of contradiction, and making isolated decisions for the sake of expediency and control is a shortcut to failure more often than success.

Risk-taking is important, for sure, but calculated risk-taking has proven to be a more successful approach in our experience. If we look up front at the objectives, tasks, mutual incentives, and required resources to deliver a project, we may well still take a significant and uncomfortable set of risks that stretch the team and limits of technology, but we are doing so knowingly and by choice. We are able to calculate the critical path of the project and be more prepared to surge resources at key points in the life of its delivery and operations.

What could we have done differently in the case above? Planned for success, anticipated the increase in organizational resource tension, and managed it to acceptable levels intentionally. We would have asked the company to transparently take these risks together, and we would have given one another the opportunity to trust, commit, and deliver.

Leaders should look at how to amplify and attenuate their individual tensions, personal and professional, to avoid their worst fear of overreacting in a tense moment.

Digging Deep

Your alarm rings, or more likely your phone; it's off to the airport again after traveling for two weeks in a row, and you're beginning to feel like your life is lived in meetings, airports, conference rooms, and hotels. Dining out is not really a treat as you are doing so either alone or in a business setting. Next up, back to the office, standing in front of your team and trying your best to be fully present while all of this logistical noise is playing in the background, burning up gray matter. Leadership is difficult enough without the constant juggling of priorities and the fact that, despite our best efforts, we are all just human and have emotions and needs as well as burning business ambitions!

How do you do this? How do you balance the tensions of your real life and your work persona? One good way to start is to just be real. Be your true self. Accept that there really is no distinction between the work you and the real you. We are not suggesting that you be as casual or familiar in a work setting as in a personal setting, but don't try to be someone you are not. If you think about it, how do you aspire to be seen by your family? Hopefully, you are aiming to just be the best version of yourself that you can muster each and every day.

In *Respect the Weeds*, we wrote about digging deep in order to survive the challenges of transformation: *At some point, you need to have the conviction to set and stick to your plan. To know when to challenge the dogma, resolve conflicts, and when to just let it go. And to take comfort that you're not alone.*

If not closely observed, organizational tensions can arise and undermine your growth and productivity. While you may not be able to prevent the rise in tension, especially when it is introduced by outside forces, you need to have your tension radar fully engaged at all times. Through the lens of intentional tension, you are better able to prepare for change and react quickly if your organization is hit with a market disruptor or the loss of a major client. You can *resprout* your value proposition and retake your rightful position in the market.

Clarify your growth vision. Map your tensions. Know how work gets done. Tune the racket. Operate in the open… culture is a verb! Those in your care will follow if you know how and where to lead them.

AUTHOR BIOGRAPHIES

Adan K. Pope is a leading authority on digital transformation, strategic technology leadership, and technology disruption, with over thirty years of career experience. Adan has served as a senior executive for many enterprises executing a digital or portfolio transformation that led to their strategic renaissance, growth, and, at times, acquisition. He has held almost every role in software technology innovation and development, from software developer to chief technology and innovation officer for some of the telecommunication industry's most innovative technology companies. Adan has also held executive leadership roles in companies serving the retail analytics/IoT, gaming, and, most recently, outsourced marketing services industries, as well as held the chief officer title for innovation, industry architecture, and strategy.

- o SVP Engineering and Applications, TAG – The Aspen Group
- o CTO/CIO/CPO, Intrado Life & Safety
- o Chief Technology and Innovation Officer, InnerWorkings
- o Chief Information Technology Officer and Chief Strategy Officer, Ciena Blue Planet
- o Chief Technology Officer, ShopperTrak
- o Vice President of Technology and CTO, Ericsson Support Solutions Business Unit
- o Chief Technology Officer and Chief Strategy Officer,
- o Telcordia Technologies
- o Head of Planning Systems Business Unit, Amdocs
- o Head of Research, Cramer Systems
- o Chief Technology Officer and Vice President of Engineering, Clear Communications

Adan has collaborated and spoken extensively on the opportunities, emerging technologies, standards, and patterns for the reimagination of the communications industry while co-authoring several patents in the process. He holds a Master of Science in Computer Science and a Master of Business Administration from North Central College in Naperville, Illinois, and a Bachelor of Science from DeVry Institute of Technology in Columbus, Ohio.

Peter J. Buonfiglio is an expert business strategist, having worked extensively in information and communications technology organizations. He has amassed a far-reaching career experience helping high-performing enterprises extract the most value from their brand, portfolio, and channels. Peter cut his teeth in market research and management consulting, which piqued his interest in organizations that were struggling to differentiate or that had lost their way. He later stepped into leadership roles that spanned from large, complex engineering organizations to startup entrepreneurial teams.

- Product Marketing Director, Intrado Life & Safety
- Brand Marketing Manager, Keysight Technologies
- Strategy and Strategic Marketing Director, Ericsson
- Strategic Marketing Director, Telcordia Technologies
- Vice President of Sales & Marketing, Fralo Plastech Mfg
- Vice President of Marketing, Rsoft Design Group
- Executive Director, Network Integrity, Bellcore
- Global Research Director, EDS Management Consulting
- Equity Research Analyst, Sherwood Securities
- Senior Consulting & Research Associate, Coopers & Lybrand

Peter graduated from Harvard University with a Bachelor of Arts in Economics. He earned a certification in Driving Strategic Impact from Columbia Business School.

Adan and Peter are also the Co-Founders of Taraxa Labs LLC. The firm was created to provide a safe space for leadership from private enterprise, the public sector, and non-profit organizations to let their guard down, to get out of their comfort zones, and to challenge the status quo. Taraxa Labs recognizes that the digital transformation game is filled with imprecision, moving targets, competing interests, security threats, and the inevitable, sometimes inexplicable, setbacks and failures that must be mitigated with a strong vision and informed judgments affecting organizations, technology, and people. Its mission is to offer leadership a sandbox for reimagination and reinvention while providing the practical tools and guidebooks to help navigate your transformation journey.

www.ingramcontent.com/pod-product-compliance
Lightning Source LLC
Chambersburg PA
CBHW050124210326
41519CB00015BA/4091